ANTH

ALTHOUGH WE HAVEN'T MET I ADMIRE YOUR DEDICATION TO WELL-BEING FROM AFAR! SORRY FOR THE DELAY IN SENDING THIS. LET'S CONNECT SOON! LIVE INSPIRED & BE SUPER HUMAN!

G.

Copyright © 2017: Ikkuma: Find Your Superhuman
Published by Ikkuma Inc.
31 Adelaide Street East
PO Box 836
Toronto, Ontario
Canada M5C 2K1

All rights reserved. No part of this publication may be reproduced, stored in a retrieval system, or transmitted in any form by any process—electronic, photocopying, recording, or otherwise—without the prior written consent of Ikkuma Inc.

Cover: Amy Ballantine
Editing: Gary LeBlanc
Illustrations: Sheila LeBlanc
Photo: Tony Cicero

Distribution:
Ikkuma Inc.
31 Adelaide Street East
PO Box 836
Toronto, Ontario
Canada M5C 2K1

ISBN: 978-1546444732

The book may contain health-related and medical-related information including statements of facts, views, opinions, recommendations, descriptions of, or references to, products, services and treatments. Such health-related and medical-related information made available by Ikkuma Inc. and the books authors and contributors is: (a) for informational purposes only; (b) not to be used or construed as a substitute for medical or any other professional advice, diagnosis, or treatment; and (c) not intended as a recommendation or endorsement of any specific tests, products, procedures, opinions or any other information. Reliance on any health-related or medical-related information in the book is solely at your own risk. Always seek the advice of your physician or other qualified health provider with any questions you may have regarding a medical or health condition. Never disregard professional medical advice or delay in seeking it because of something you have read in this book. You agree that all risk associated with the use of, or reliance on, any of the information in this book rests with you. You further agree that neither the author nor the contributor nor Ikkuma Inc. shall be responsible or liable, directly or indirectly, in any way for any loss or damage of any kind incurred as a result of, or in connection with, your use of, or reliance on, any such information.

Dedicated to Brad MacMillan

With the passing years, I am reminded how time waits for no one. The more distracted we become, the quicker time seems to pass.

It's been seven years since Brad breathed his last breath. Each year that goes by represents yet another year stolen from Brad. Another year that Brad would have given anything to experience. I remember Brad sharing one wish just before he died, "... to know what it feels like to have one more healthy day."

As a society, (for the most part) we seem to take our health for granted. We haven't yet been gifted the clarity that mortality provides.

Brad was my gift. The time I spent with Brad forever changed my perspective, and in turn, my life. I miss Brad. I feel guilty that he had to suffer so much, while I am still able to continue my journey.

One day I hope to meet Brad once again, in another reality. But not yet. Until then, I strive to keep Brad's spirit alive. This is one such attempt.

Cheers!

Acknowledgments

Writing this was a journey out of my comfort zone. I'd like to thank the people critical in making it happen:

My business partner Brian Coones. What can I say... There wouldn't be a book without Brian's vision. My brother, always.

Angelina and I bounced concepts around ad nauseam. I can't think of anybody with whom I would rather better to collaborate.

Kennedy Lodato for being the fitness guru.

Sarah Moritz got me through countless moments of doubt and was the editor behind the scenes.

My sisters! Jacqueline for her engagement on the project from day one, and Sheila for the spiritual illustrations that truly pay homage to Inuit culture.

Don for taking the time to be a fantastic sounding board and ambassador.

The rest of my family and friends. When everyone believes in you more than you believe in yourself, you don't want to let them down.

THANK YOU!

"Gratitude"—The key to being grateful is reviewing what you have. I am grateful for the incredible people who have helped me on this amazing transformation.

Table of Contents

Acknowledgments v
Foreword 1
A Personal Letter 5
The Journey 7
So, What's Broken? 14

Section ONE
Part One—How the Body Works 18

Our Body's Fuel 19
Food Building Blocks—Macronutrients 21
Hormones… The Body's Chemical Messengers 28
Now It's Feeding Time! 30
Digestion 31
I Have a 'Gut' Feeling 35

Part Two—Disease… Know Thy Enemy 39

Key Precursors to Disease 40
Common Diseases 47
Cancer 49
Diabetes 53
Cardiovascular Disease and Stroke 55

Section TWO
Part One: Foods To 'Live' By
(Ikkuma Translation: Feeding the Fire) 58

Key Foods to Eat   61
To Be or Not to Be Organic   75
So What About Supplements?   90
Eat Your Power Foods   101
Alkaline Versus Acidic Foods... WTF?   102

Part Two: Foods To 'Drive' By
(Ikkuma Translation: The Fire Is Starting to Fade) 108

Section THREE
Toxins... The Ugly Truth
(Ikkuma Translation: 'Get That Tire Out of the Fire!') 124

The Marvels of Modern Medicine?   139

Section FOUR
Keeping the Body Tuned Up
(Ikkuma Translation: Stoking the Fire) 152

    Stress... The Silent Killer   153
    Sleep... The Body's Time to Heal   158
    Fitness... Use It or Lose It   164
    It Has Always Been Your Choice   182

Bibliography   189
End Notes   191

Foreword

I got to know Gary several years ago during a time when one of his best friends was diagnosed with cancer. Being an engineer, Gary tried to grasp the issues surrounding cancer and understand the latest thoughts concerning prevention and treatment. Eventually, Gary became interested in identifying how the body works and how it is impacted by external factors such as the environment, nutrition, exercise, and so on.

When I first heard that Gary was going to write a book about health I was extremely pleased and excited to see the final copy. I had already sat through two seminars by Gary where he covered his thoughts on exercise, nutrition, and supplements. Not only was the information interesting and valuable but Gary's understanding of the research when answering questions during the seminars was extremely impressive. I have personally taken his advice on exercise, supplements, and diet and have been pleased with the results.

What I appreciate about the book is the amount of work that Gary has put into understanding the latest thinking on how our body functions, how it processes nutrients and what each of us can do to avoid illness.

My personal philosophy is that we need to have balance in our lives whether that be work, fitness, developing our mind or having fun. It all eventually boils down to where we choose to spend our time and how do we do things in the most efficient way possible to obtain the results we desire. All of us are individuals on this journey of life. We need to take control of what we do with our time, how we treat others, and also importantly, how we treat ourselves.

As Gary points out, if someone does not take an interest in their well-being they cannot expect someone else, their family or the government to do it for them. They will live with the consequences. We only have one body and one brain, so why not take reasonable actions to ensure that we have a functional mind and body and a positive attitude.

I find the amount of information that is available about diet, supplements, exercise, the impact of toxins and what we put on our body, sleep, and so on is not only confusing but extremely time-consuming to sift through. What I love about Gary's book is that he has taken an unbiased view and spent countless hours researching a wide variety of topics which he has summarized in a very readable fashion so that we can all have a good understanding of how things work and what we can be doing to optimize our health.

For anyone to do this on their own, it would take hundreds if not thousands of hours to review the latest research to sift through what makes sense, what is fact-based and what is opinion, and analytically come to a conclusion about what is best for ourselves. Gary has done this for us. I have no doubt there are other opinions in specific fields and our knowledge in this area will continue to evolve and grow. However, I am confident that the conclusions Gary has reached are based on his unbiased, detailed research.

To the readers of this book, if you ever have the pleasure of meeting Gary and listening to one of his presentations, he is not only passionate but also very generous with his time in talking to people and answering questions to make them more educated in these fields. Moreover, he is a living example of how to be in great shape and practices what he preaches.

One of the most important parts of anyone's life is to be positive. We have so much to live for, so why not invest the time to understand how to maximize the functioning of our body and mind? This leads to a healthy spirit. It is relatively easy to live proactively in a way that keeps us optimally functioning in both body and spirit. It is amazing the number of people who show great discipline and attention to detail when they are at work—why not do the same for our most important asset—ourselves? I look forward to seeing if Gary can produce some natural products that live up to the standards written about in the book such that we can eat and drink what is healthy and has been well researched.

I hope that you enjoy the book as much as I did. Additionally, I hope you gain the knowledge and motivation to apply whatever makes sense for you and that you live a happier, healthier life with less risk of developing a disease.

Gary, thank you for putting this book together. I know I was one of the people encouraging you to do so, such that we all could learn from it.

Don Walker
Chief Executive Officer
Magna International Inc.

A Personal Letter

Dear friend,

My name is Gary LeBlanc. I'm an east-coast boy, now living in the heart of Canada.

I had a fairly typical Canadian upbringing. We were a middle-class family that had what we needed. But childhood was a constant struggle. I had a debilitating stutter and ears that stuck out like Dumbo (as per kids in the playground). Growing up was beyond tricky. Actually, more often than not, it defeated me. It was the source of unyielding anxiety.

I believe our consciousness is the function of our genetics, and is influenced by every single sight, smell, touch, taste, and sound that we encounter. Be it consciously, or subconsciously, absorbing the information. It all becomes part of us.

My consciousness was heavily shaped during my youth. The constant insecurity-breeding-ridicule, stemming from my stuttering and big ears, was destined to instigate a powerful response, a counterpoint. It did indeed.

Life after childhood was fuelled by the singular pursuit of 'success.' I was consumed with comparing my accomplishments to others. I needed constant validation. I was tired of living in fear and feeling inadequate. I can now clearly see how my life became a direct result of the bullying.

Health in my 20's and early 30's was motivated by the need to look good, while not necessarily living well. Yet this need to look good began to expose snippets of a deeper truth. Via osmosis, I began to connect the dots. I began to understand the impetus for the lifestyle choices I was making. I began to realize that looking good and being healthy didn't need to be mutually exclusive. They could both be a part of a more-evolved lifestyle. This newfound perspective inspired new beliefs, and behaviours. I decided that I couldn't continue on my vanity-centric trajectory any longer.

See, the challenge isn't knowing how to live with vitality. The challenge lies in motivating people to choose differently. This book doesn't present a technical solution. Its singular goal is to inspire, inform, and motivate people to change.

That's it. All we need to do is motivate and enable over seven billion humans to choose differently (if their circumstances permit). Call it lofty. Call it naive. Maybe it is. You may be reading this and judge my goals as unrealistic. But what harm is there in believing that we can do it. One thing I can guarantee is that such a lofty goal demands my highest level of energy and belief. So regardless of my degree of success, I can't lose if 100% of my consciousness is that focused. And yes, 100% of my consciousness is that focused.

I'm a Mechanical Engineer by trade and a Life Engineer by purpose. Engineers solve complex problems. Armed with thousands of hours of research and my partner Dr. Angelina Riopel's expertise, let us help you solve the most pressing problem of all, living your best life.

Success for me would be to inspire you to become more aware of your choices, to focus on living a happy and healthy life, and to enable you to share your unique gift with the world. I thank you for making it this far. I will be ever so grateful if you choose to take the rest of this journey with me.

Or even better, if you prefer Shakespeare, 'Once more unto the breach, dear friends, once more.'

Regards,

Gary

> "Time is the coin of your life. It is the only coin you have, and only you can determine how it will be spent. Be careful lest you let other people spend it for you."
> —Carl Sandberg, American Poet

The Journey

For some of us, the journey is short and wrought with suffering. For others, the journey is a long celebration of life. In all cases, the journey is all we have. There is no panacea when we reach the end. The moment - the here and now - is all we have. For my dear friend Brad, this couldn't have been more true.

Brad was a strapping middle-aged man. 6'3". Played football in university. Was raised on a farm. Moved to Toronto. Became part of the scene. Worked out. Had fun. Typical.

Although typical, he was also unique, as in one-in-a-million unique. He had this thing where you could see when he was thinking hard. His eyes would drift to the top right, looking at the corner of the room as if there would be some divine message tucked away. He would often hum while he was thinking. The hamster wheel was turning hard. When he finally—after a few seconds—figured out what he wanted to say, he would hum, and his hands would begin to move erratically. Then he would explain. You would have expected a filtered response after such apparent deliberation. You'd be wrong.

Brad more often than not put his foot in his mouth. Sometimes it was funny. Sometimes it was frustrating as hell. Like the time he told a friend's ex-girlfriend that his friend had moved on. He went on telling her how happy his friend was and how the new girlfriend was perfect for him. While he was saying this, the poor girl's face underwent dozens of contortions. Brad never meant to be malicious. He was just bringing her up to speed and failed to realize that she might not want to hear it.

But that was Brad. Everyone knew him for that. They also knew him as the life of the party, a guy with a pure heart, and someone too honest for his own good. People who knew Brad loved Brad. I loved Brad.

...

I was having a drink at a cafe in Amsterdam when Brad called me. Two days before, I was in Geneva, scheduled to come home. A major volcanic eruption in the heart of Iceland grounded European flights for days, preventing me from returning home. I decided to drive to Amsterdam, providing the option for a direct flight home. Amsterdam became my home for the next five days. Under normal circumstances, this wouldn't have been a bad thing. Normal circumstances these were not.

Brad rarely made phone calls. Since his stage-4 lymphoma returned, after a brief remission, he only picked up the phone to text. So when I received the call in Amsterdam, hearing him on the other end was a shock.

'Hey Gary, what time are you coming to visit me?'

'Brad! Sorry bud. Do you remember me mentioning that I needed to go to Europe for a quick meeting? I should have been home by now, but a bizarre volcanic eruption has delayed my trip home for a few days.'

'What time will you be by the hospital?'

By that time in his treatment, the drugs were messing with Brad's memory. It wasn't registering that I wouldn't be seeing him in a few hours. After four years of battling cancer, Brad's body and mind were weary. After four years of powerful chemo, blood transfusions, and repeated draining of his lungs, his body was not his own anymore. He was now dealing with uncontrollable bowel movements, and bouts of horribly restrained breathing. A positive prognosis for Brad was fleeting.

'Brad, I don't know when I'll be home. I'm sorry buddy.'

I cried. Brad's journey had taken a wrong turn. Trying to make sense of Brad's suffering was moot at that point. No human ever deserves that level of pain.

...

On Mother's Day, 2010, at 9:20 am, Brad took his last breath. Fittingly, Brad was alone.

Before his death, he was embarrassed to be seen in such a frail state. He would only allow myself and his immediate family to visit. He didn't want people remembering him as a skeleton covered by a thin layer of skin. He wanted people to remember the football player who could party with the best of them. The 6'3", sandy blond, Canadian boy.

Brad's journey was over. Mine was about to begin.

...

Brad's passing was not normal. It wasn't supposed to happen that way. He had too much life left to live. So what happened? How does it make any sense that someone so young and healthy falls apart?

Life's a game of numbers. I get it. It could happen to anyone. I get it. But the 'numbers' argument is precisely why I had to try and enlighten people to make better decisions, to be more aware. There are too many Brad's. With all the advice in the world available to us at the press of a button, why are there that many Brads? Maybe the solution needed more of an engineer's perspective.

Nearly 50% of males will get cancer in their lifetime; women fair slightly better at just over a third. The most alarming thing is the seemingly indiscriminate fashion cancer attacks. It's an all ages condition.

I'm won't start preaching, no time for that, but health trends need to change. Now. Unfortunately, this isn't a fair fight. There are too many powerful multinational companies working against us whose motive is solely financial. They base their innocence on ignorance and plausible deniability. While deep down they know they're not acting in the best interest of peoples' health. Their share price is the only metric that influences their decisions.

But we can demand more. The democratization of information has finally given us the ammunition to drive change. We can be proactive in managing our well-being, our future, our journey. But alas, our Western lifestyle has created a formidable adversary. Our bodies haven't evolved to handle the grueling obstacle course we put it through. There are now too many unknowns to solve. Despite all our medical advances, whatever technology we've thrown at the 'problem' has fallen short. Yes, we're getting closer to solving the code of some major diseases with genomics, biotech, and nanotechnology, but we're playing Space Invaders with one million invaders descending on each of us at the same time. We can't win by letting others solve the problem. We need to take responsibility.

Unless we start to become more self-aware and understand that we don't make the rules, things won't change. There will be more Brads.

...

Ikkuma—pronounced ee-koo-ma—means fire in the Northern Canadian language Inuktitut. That was the name my partner, and I chose for the company that would address this lofty problem. We chose this name for two reasons: the Inuit have a strong reverence for nature, and fire represents rejuvenation.

There's no more apt metaphor than a forest fire for what Ikkuma aspires to achieve. I watched a documentary on forest fires recently. In great detail, it chronicled what happens to a forest when a fire takes hold. For a diseased and dead forest, fire is its only hope. Within hours of fire taking hold, the forest releases the energy is has absorbed over decades. The previously dead forest is brought back to life. It's magical.

As a society, have we not become diseased? Have we not become something less than what we are capable of? With the average person suffering with disease for the last ten years of their life, are we not the dying forest? Are we not in need of drastic measures? Nothing incremental will change the ending to this story.

There are no quick fixes for what we (as a society) have become. Catalyzing our transformation will take much more than a match or a lightning strike. It will take a monumental shift in awareness. Perseverance will be needed to fuel this awareness. Just as the growth of a muscle is a function of its time under tension, society will become more aware via education and time. Unfortunately for many of us, disease will reach our door prematurely because we didn't take action soon enough. But there's good news.

If you choose to make changes today, you can, like the forest, begin to see changes immediately. In a matter of hours, your body will start its transformation.

This early in the book I don't want to scare you off with science but there are two main reasons to have faith in how quickly your body will benefit from even the smallest changes.

The first is epigenetics—the study of non-genetic influences on gene expression. Simply stated, our environment, the decisions we make, every single thought, event, or encounter, has the potential to affect how a gene is expressed—resulting in both good and bad outcomes. A gene we want to remain 'dormant' may be activated or expressed under certain conditions, such as poor diet or stress. And vice versa.

While altering our genetic code (i.e., DNA) may happen from generation to generation, we can influence our gene expression hour-to-hour, day-to-day, month-to-month. So what we do matters. A lot.

The second reason to believe in the immediate impact of your lifestyle may surprise you. Your microbiome—the microorganisms (mostly good and bad bacteria) in your gut—is in constant communication with the rest of your body. There are an estimated 10-100 trillion bacteria cells, representing dozens of different bacterial strains, in your gut. Science is only now understanding the critical, symbiotic mechanisms that are influenced by this area of our body. From mood to nutrient absorption, the lifestyle you choose today will affect your health tomorrow.

There are too many reasons to choose healthy habits to remain ignorant. The barriers to making better decisions are becoming increasingly surmountable. Let's get busy eliminating the barriers to knowing how to improve your lifestyle, and give you what you need to know with minimal time investment.

What will it take? What's your motivation?

Maybe you're just giving this a go, maybe you're dedicated to absorbing every last detail, or maybe you're somewhere in between. Regardless, of your motivation, I have made it my purpose for you to *want* to take this journey with me.

The days for half-measures are done. What I strive to do is change your consciousness. I strive to arm you with the insight needed to extend your lifespan. I strive to give you more quality years. Because as they say, it's not the years in your life, it's the life in your years. I call that vitality.

Before getting into the nuts and bolts, we need to set some ground rules. While we could tweak the specifics for each and every person reading this, the foundation for vibrant health remains the same for everybody. There is a healthy balance in your life that represents the best shot you have to live your best life possible.

Liken this to a credit card. You're responsible for paying off your debts. The more you spend, the harder it will be to pay off those debts. Ideally, you don't want to carry your balance forward. You want to cover your debts off on a regular basis. The longer you carry debt, the more damage it will wreak on your body, not unlike the accumulation of interest on your credit card. I refer to my health balance as my Ikkuma account.

The trick is knowing your limits. What's the upper-limit your body can handle? What's a comfortable balance for you? What do you have the discipline to manage? How much interest can your body handle? I can't answer that for you. But I can show you how to learn this for yourself.

Once you become more aware, it's this self-awareness that should dictate what you do next. You will better understand how hard it is to pay off the debt of a weekend binge or a sloppy business meal on a trip. Better decisions will become second nature. But you need to gain a minimal amount of knowledge to help guide you on your journey. You will need to invest time and effort.

Are you willing to invest? How much are you willing to pay to live one more day, one more week, one more year? What are you willing to do to live your best life possible?

...

Being sick sucks. It's ugly. It can be hell on earth. Heck, just having the flu feels like life is coming to an end. But when the effects of bad decisions aren't as immediate as a stomach virus, the challenge becomes linking the short-term cause to the long-term effect. See, the causes are happening now, and the effects will most likely become apparent when it's too late for you to react.

Inaction isn't acceptable. The connection needs to be understood now. We need to connect the dots. We need to bridge the 'present' cause with the 'future' effect. We need to do this now. I'll do my best to motivate you, but only you can choose to be proactive.

I'm asking you to trust me. I'm asking you to trust that investing a day or so reading this book will result in a one-thousand-fold benefit. Every cell in my consciousness wants this for you. I can honestly say this because I believe that everybody deserves to live up to their unique potential.

None of us chose our circumstances at birth. From birth until this very moment, life has been a game of dominoes. We react based on how we were made, how we were treated, and what we experienced. Regardless of the pain we're harboring from our past, we deserve to live to our potential. We all have a unique gift that needs the best part of us to come to the plate, day-in-day-out.

I want this for you. I want this for me.

...

I've been on one hell of a journey. There have been some highs and some dark lows. So, I'm not speaking from a place of judgment. I'm speaking from a place of empathy. I'm just lucky enough to have been gifted the insight that can only be experienced from personal pain. You could say that my buddy Brad was my Messiah.

I didn't know it at the time. I couldn't predict how the dots of Brad's suffering would connect. I couldn't visualize the puzzle so early in my transformation. All I can tell you is that when you start to become more aware... when you start to accept that you're worth it... when you start to accept that you deserve to share your unique gift with the world... only then will you be on your journey. Until that point, you'll be a victim of the prevailing winds, like a feather in a hurricane, powerless.

I want you to live your purpose, to express your unique gift. I want to be impacted by each and every one of you. I've taken a risk living my purpose. All I ask is that you give me the opportunity to help you live yours.

In my humble way, maybe through mind and body health, I can motivate you to take the risk. Again, this is a lofty goal but wouldn't that be something. Wouldn't a shift in consciousness be incredible?

Yes, it would.

So, What's Broken?

"Beginnings"—The journey you are about to embark on is unique, but every journey does have a Beginning. Let's begin…

"It is no measure of health to be well adjusted to a profoundly sick society."
—JIDDU KRISHNAMURTI, 20TH CENTURY INDIAN PHILOSOPHER

Throughout the book, I will often refer to the "Western" diet epidemic. This epidemic includes both Americans and Canadians alike. I'll also quote facts that may highlight one country or the other. Both our countries are facing the same challenges in varying degrees. To put the present situation in context, let's look at some shocking stats.

While America spends more per capita on healthcare than any other country in the world (nearly double that of Germany, who is next in line):

- over two thirds of the population is overweight, that is, a body mass index (BMI) over 25
- over one third is obese (BMI over 30)
- over 25 million Americans have diabetes[1]
- over 75 million are prediabetic[2]
- the American Cancer Society reports that over 1 in 2 American males will get cancer in their lifetime; with females faring slightly better at over 1 in 3[3]

- diabetes (mostly Type-II) has been skyrocketing—strongly correlated with the obesity epidemic. Over one out of every thirteen Americans now have some form of diabetes. Of those, nearly 30% are not even aware they have it. The health costs related to this epidemic in the U.S. is approximately $245 billion[4]

BMI is a measure of obesity. Over 25 BMI is classified as overweight—e.g., someone at 5'9" weighing 170 lbs—while over 30 BMI is classified as obese—e.g., someone at the same height but weighing 192 lbs. Following today's obesity trends, by 2030 nearly half of America's citizens will be obese.

Not even our children are spared. Nearly a third of America's children are considered overweight, while 15% are obese.

And this isn't just America's problem. Accordingly to Dr. Ezzati (Imperial College professor in London), in 2008 one-third of the global population was overweight—double the rates observed in 1980[5].

This is both disappointing and disgusting at the same time. This isn't about vanity. It's about a lost generation. A generation lost to disease. We can't afford to continue as-is.

Pharmaceuticals and Processed Food... Modern Society's Profit-Driven Response?

The main response to our diseased society lies on the backs of pharmaceuticals. Fact: Pharmaceutical companies can't make money unless you are buying and relying on their drugs. While unsuspecting consumers are sold on drugs as the solution to every health problem, they are rarely informed that these conditions could have been avoided. To make matters worse, these drugs we rely on cause further adverse reactions that then need to be addressed. This translates into over 100,000 American deaths (due to prescription drugs) annually[6]. So why is symptom management our focus vs. putting our energies toward prevention?

Not only do we over-medicate but reliance on mechanically-made foods is at an all-time high. Despite the genius behind nature's design of food, we have brushed it aside, allowing ourselves to be romanced by packaged-food health claims and convenience.

The hard truth is that multinational food companies have a duty to shareholders. While values may vary from company to company, profit remains their primary driver. Do you think that any of the major processed food companies would help out if you couldn't pay the medical bills from treating your diabetes? They wouldn't.

This fiduciary shareholder duty influences their marketing tactics as well. Marketing their often-sugar-laden products to children has become a pandemic. With tens of billions of dollars spent in advertising, parents are no match for the coffers of food companies. At some point, shouldn't we all be ashamed? When did society decide to value profits above the health of our children?

The simple truth is that the basis of healthy living lies in the recognition that nature has laid everything out for us. Throughout Find Your SuperHuman you will see one recurring theme—we've had the solution to a vibrant and healthy life all this time. But, we have chosen to ignore it. As Paulo Coelho showed us in *The Alchemist*, sometimes the treasure lies right under our noses.

Part ONE
How the Body Works

(Ikkuma Translation: Building The Fire)

Ignorance can be bliss. Not (often) feeling the damage we're doing to our bodies makes motivation to change that much more elusive. Compounding this general ignorance is our false sense of security regarding our health, because the effects of bad habits are rarely immediate. When you fail to exercise, or binge eat, you aren't notified that your probability of disease has just gone up. When you breathe in artificial air fresheners, it's impossible to see the millions of adverse reactions they have on your body.

We need to be proactive and better understand the rules of the game, to make better decisions. Having a basic understanding of how the body works is the first step in deciding to take control of your wellness. Although you can implement positive habits without understanding the 'why', the why will provide motivation when your willpower is being tested. Still, some people don't need to understand the why, they just want the 'what' and the 'how'. That's perfectly fine. But for those who want to be informed, bear with me through the theory in this section, because it will drive home the necessity for change. A little knowledge goes a long way.

What you will read is logical. Common sense. You might even know some of it. Yet, for many of us, the body represents an undiscovered country.

This section isn't meant to provide you infinite detail. I aim to give you a foundation upon which to make better choices for your body going forward. I've done all the heavy lifting. You just need to kick back and start learning about how your intricate body works.

Our Body's Fuel

Brief History

The agricultural revolution, which occurred approximately 12,000 years ago, set the stage for a monumental shift in human evolution. In the book, *The Paleo Solution*[1], Cordain discusses the effects that this huge change in lifestyle had on our physical evolution and health.

Along with many others, Cordain contends that before this era, human beings were as tall—and healthier than—present day humans. The rates of degenerative diseases were a fraction of what we see today. Their skin was more youthful, and they thrived physically. Furthermore, societies that have remained hunter-gatherers have consistently demonstrated better health than their farming counterparts, with lower mortality rates, fewer cavities, and longer life.

Now let's fast forward to the 21st century; after 12,000 years of progress, do we place value on what we feed our bodies? If what North Americans spend on food expenditures is any indication, we haven't. In 2010, Americans spent under 10% of their disposable income on eating; with approximately 5.5% going towards eating in the home, and 4% towards eating out[2]. The percentage Americans spend eating in the home is less than half of most countries, with Italy and France spending nearly three times more than Americans.

These percentages are significantly lower than those in the 1930's, where nearly 25% of Americans' disposable income went to food. Obviously, there have been advances in food production productivity, but this represents a small percentage of the decline. Western society (specifically North Americans) has chosen to produce and consume cheaper food of poor nutritional quality, over buying high-quality, non-genetically modified foods, void of contaminants. Although we may proportionately spend less on food in North America versus other parts of the world, we are one of the most overweight regions.

As reported in the HBO documentary series, *The Weight of a Nation*, the daily caloric consumption in the U.S. has risen in the past few decades from under 2200 calories to approximately 2700 calories. This alarming increase of nearly 25% is entirely due to what we eat—cheap, high caloric food—and our sedentary lifestyles. We have become a society that values iPhones over our future health. You rarely hear people complain about the price of their iPhone, but people are appalled by the relatively high cost of organic food.

Really? We spend a pittance on our food and then justify going on-the-cheap by convincing ourselves that a little pesticide exposure is alright. What the heck, the corporations selling the pesticides say it's safe.

Not only is our cheap food essentially void of nutrition, but it hides the true cost. The subsidies—government financial support—on certain crops and environmental costs are not built into the price when you're paying less than a dollar for a two-liter bottle of soda. Therein lies the irony: despite the fact it's making us sicker, processed and genetically modified food hoards the lion's share of all food subsidies. These subsidies support commodities, crop insurance, conservation and disaster protection—and most of these crops are genetically modified. In the U.S., out of the $277 billion in subsidies paid out between 1995–2011, corn, wheat, cotton, and soy represented approximately $175 billion of the total payout. As will be shown later in the book, the gross majority of these crops are born of genetically modified seeds.

These modern processed and refined foods are taking a toll on society:

- their empty, excessive calories are harmful and induce fat storage
- they are riddled with artificial ingredients and chemicals that damage our bodies, on both a microscopic and macroscopic level
- health care costs associated with this Westernized diet are skyrocketing, with some experts predicting that obesity will soon become our #1 health care cost (if we aren't there already)

This trend of overconsumption and reliance on cheap food is not sustainable for a healthy society. The only way to improve our health is by focusing on both the quantity and the quality of the food we consume, favoring foods that are nutritionally dense (i.e., loaded with nutrients and minerals). With society's present mindset that goal may seem unattainable, but I can assure you it's quite straightforward.

Food Building Blocks—Macronutrients

The word 'macronutrient' doesn't mean *macro* as in a triple cheeseburger. I'm figuring you know that, but surprisingly two-thirds of the population hasn't grasped the real definition. Macronutrient refers to the big three types of nutrients: carbohydrates, fats, and proteins. I will include fiber in there as an honorable mention since it is key to a healthy diet.

Carbohydrates

Carbohydrates are found in foods ranging from spinach to pasta and from beans to cereal. The families of carbohydrates are referred to as saccharides (i.e., sugars)—mono (one), di (two), and polysaccharides (many sugars). Carbohydrates are processed in the body and reduced to a monosaccharide called glucose. Glucose is your body's preferred source of fuel. Although much of the body can burn alternative sources of fuel for energy, the brain, and red blood cell production rely on glucose.

Although necessary for energy production, excess carbohydrates—what you ingest by downing that chocolate sundae—elevate your blood sugar and prompt an insulin spike, both of which can become harmful to the body. When eaten with fiber, protein, and fats, carbohydrates absorb more slowly, tempering our insulin response. Managing our production of insulin is key to maintaining a healthy lifestyle.

Fats

Fats are often misunderstood. Contrary to what has been indoctrinated in the public's consciousness since the mid-20th century, fat does not necessarily make you fat. Several studies have shown that even high fat intake does not promote cardiovascular disease or obesity in many individuals.

One classic study, *The Seven Countries Study* by Ancel Keys, essentially absolved fats of their unsubstantiated link to heart disease. The study was then handed over to the McGovern committee—formed in the U.S. from 1968–77, tasked with addressing the rising concern of hunger and malnutrition. For the most part, the committee ignored the findings, maintaining their attack on fats in the media. Despite fats being vilified throughout history, what has the potential for promoting excess body fat are simple carbs.

Fats are an essential part of our physiology. Our brains are predominantly made of fat, and our cell membranes are composed of fat. Fat-soluble vitamins, such as vitamins E, A, D and K, need fat in order to be absorbed by our intestinal tract. And yes, fat does make a lot of things taste better!

There are three main types of fat:

- saturated
- monounsaturated
- polyunsaturated

I'll give a dishonorable mention to (predominantly) man-made trans fats, which I will explain later.

Saturated fats, such as coconut oil and some animal fat, are typically inert and can last a long time in ambient conditions. Monounsaturated fats are fats with one double bond (don't worry about the significance of the double bond, we'll just refer to it for identification purposes). Examples of foods mainly composed of monounsaturated fats are avocados and olive oil.

Polyunsaturated fats have more than one double bond. This is where we find our omega-3s—often associated with fish oil—and omega-6s.

i. Saturated Fats

Ironically, saturated fats—demonized decades ago, and often supplanted by the much more unhealthy trans fats—are a necessary component to our diet. You can find saturated fats in several different foods, namely, dairy, meat, and certain oils, such as coconut oil.

It baffles me how the public is advised to avoid saturated fats, despite having so many influential roles in the body. They are crucial for cell membrane function, increase satiety (that "full" feeling), help transport fat-soluble vitamins (A, E, D, and K), and are building blocks for several hormones.

Why is it that the public was advised to avoid saturated fats? Because public health warnings like these are often meant to protect the interests of food-manufacturing companies. This is why it is so important to do your research, rather than blindly putting faith in advertising.

The much bigger problem occurs when you replace saturated fats with carbohydrates; especially processed and refined carbohydrates, such as starches and sugars. Over-processed grains fit into this category as well, in that they are easily and completely digested, much like sugars. In fact, your body can barely tell the difference between most sliced bread and a can of soda. Shortly, I'll elaborate on what happens to your body when you overload on carbohydrates; the cycle of insulin resistance, metabolic syndrome (including obesity), and its adverse effects on your cholesterol profile.

While saturated fats are key to a healthy diet, you need to exercise moderation, meaning foods like red meat should not be part of your daily diet, and you should avoid excessive tropical vegetable oils.

Let me leave you with some other advice for consuming saturated fats:

- Coconut Oil: Use coconut oil instead of olive oil for cooking, as it has a higher burning point. When you cook with extra-virgin olive oil at temperatures above its burning point (~ 325 degrees F), it oxidizes and develops carcinogenic, cholesterol-forming compounds.
- Organic Butter: Avoid margarine (contains hydrogenated vegetable oils—trans fats) and substitute it with organic butter. The whole push for margarine in the mid-1900s was misguided. Trans fats have been found to contribute to several diseases, such as cancer, and hormone imbalances[4].
- Animal Fats: These include red meat, chicken, dairy, and eggs. All have varying amounts of saturated fat content, with red meat containing the highest concentration. While dairy does not need to be included in a healthy diet, if you do consume dairy, try making sure it's organic and preferably raw (unpasteurized). Unfortunately, unpasteurized milk is tough to find in North America, as it is strictly controlled.

ii. Mono- and Polyunsaturated Fats

Before getting to the star of the show—polyunsaturated fats—let's give a very brief overview of monounsaturated fats.

Monounsaturated fats are an essential part of a healthy diet. You can find large amounts of this fat in red meat, nuts, and fruit high in fat, such as avocados and olives. Monounsaturated fats have been shown to reduce LDL (bad) cholesterol and—good for heart health. Ideally, about 10–15% of your diet should include this beneficial fat.

When people mention polyunsaturated fats they are often referring to omega-3s and omega-6s. Omega-3s are essential fats that play a key role in cognitive function, are anti-inflammatory (inflammation—which will be discussed in detail later in the book—can lead to a very extensive list of illnesses and diseases), and help block angiogenesis (the formation of new blood vessels, which is vital for cancer growth).

The two most important omega-3s are EPA and DHA, while the third omega-3, ALA, garners less attention.

Omega-3s are not prominent in the typical Western diet (also known as SAD, or the Standard American Diet). Fish is a good source, but most commercial fish is high in mercury. Mercury is a severe toxin and accumulates in fatty tissue—leaving the brain especially vulnerable. When possible, choose small, wild fish instead, as they are good sources of omega-3s and low in mercury. (I've included a handy reference table in the *Foods To 'Live' By* section). If you choose a supplement, krill oil or other wild, cold-processed fish oils are good alternatives.

Omega-6s—in foods ranging from whole foods, such as nuts and seeds, to processed foods—are abundant in our diet. Although necessary in the right quantities, omega-6s can be proinflammatory (i.e., prompt an inflammatory response), and require higher levels of omega-3 to normalize their effects.

One key point to remember is that omega-3s and omega-6s share the same enzymes needed for their conversion. That is why ratios of omega-3s to omega-6s in the range of 1:1 or 1:2 are crucial. Unfortunately, typical ratios in the Western diet are approximately 1:15. Clearly, we have work to do.

Cholesterol Deserves an Honorable Mention

The cholesterol we are used to hearing about is, in fact, a mix of proteins, fatty acids, glycerol, and the molecule cholesterol. Cholesterol is key to proper cell function, in that it is necessary for the permeability of the cell wall (important for nutrients entering the cell), and acts as a Band-Aid for damage that occurs to the arterial wall. Cholesterol is mainly produced in the liver, but is also produced in the brain.

Cholesterol has been a hot topic for decades. For the most part, it has been misunderstood and vilified; often associated with cardiovascular disease and stroke. In reality, your total cholesterol should not be the predominant indication of increased risk for these conditions. Ideally, one should scrutinize the ratio between good (HDL) and bad (LDL) cholesterol.

That's what I find incredibly unnerving. How can all these 'experts' be wrong? Because that's the propaganda they were being fed. We need to muddle through all the latest-and-greatest claims and rhetoric to find the truth. The problem is—with a world filled with special interest groups and social media feeds—facts are becoming harder and harder to spot.

Since cholesterol is such a hot topic, let's investigate high-density lipoprotein (i.e., HDL or good cholesterol) and low-density lipoprotein (i.e., LDL or bad cholesterol) in a little more detail.

i. "Good" Cholesterol

High-Density Lipoprotein or HDL is a form of cholesterol that transports fats and cholesterol in the body, back to the liver for processing. Think of it as a the first step in a closed system, working in conjunction with low-density lipoprotein (LDL).

ii. "Bad" Cholesterol

Low-Density Lipoproteins or LDLs are not all bad, as they convey fats (lipids and glycerol) and cholesterol from the liver to different parts of the body. This process provides fuel and functional elements for proper cell operation. The preferred structure of LDL cholesterol is large and low density, which flows freely through your bloodstream aiding cells in need. The problem arises with the small, higher density LDLs, as they get stuck in the crevices of our damaged arteries, inciting an immune response. This causes further damage and inflammation to the arterial wall. These higher density LDL's typically arise from a diet riddled with processed foods and refined carbohydrates.

Recent animal research suggests that it is oxidized cholesterol that is the true culprit of inflammation, causing arterial plaque and related damage[5]. Your arteries are lined with endothelial cells, which have receptors that pick up the oxidized cholesterol. Unfortunately, your immune system has bad judgment and recognizes the oxidized cholesterol as invaders. Macrophages—cells instrumental in defense—are sent to clean up the mess, leaving behind a pile of inflammation.

Oxidized cholesterol is the result of overheated vegetable oils (such as canola, and corn oils) mixing with oxygen. You should not consume overheated vegetables oils at any time. Moreover, most of these oils are derived from genetically modified seeds. The majority of people cook with these oils, not realizing that overheating leads to oxidation, which renders them potentially carcinogenic. So, that extra-virgin olive oil you've been cooking with is possibly doing more harm than heart-saving good. A better choice for cooking is organic coconut oil (a saturated fat), which has a higher burning point. And remember, you should never be frying at high heat, regardless of the oil you are using. Frying at high temperatures can take any oil past its burning, or oxidation point. Frying at low to medium heat is ideal.

Ikkuma INFO: FREE RADICALS

We are often bombarded with warnings concerning the detriments of free radicals. Atoms—the building block of any organic element—(typically) have paired positive and negative charges. Free radicals are atoms with unpaired electrons. They attempt to steal an electron from atoms with whom they react. This can be a good or bad thing, depending on the type of free radical and with what it reacts. Due to their volatility—stealing electrons from other compounds, initiating inflammation—excess amounts of certain free radicals can cause cellular damage and be extremely detrimental to our health. They have been linked to increased risk of cancer, stroke, and heart disease. Regarding cancer specifically, free radicals are thought to react with

DNA. These reactions can lead to cellular mutations, which begin the chain reaction of cancer. The key is to keep them under control by improving your diet with phytochemicals and antioxidants (effectively neutralizing free radicals), reducing toxins, and dealing with stress... basically, everything I will try to help you improve upon in this book.

Here are a few ways to optimize your cholesterol levels:

- eat a lot of raw foods, including healthy fats, such as avocados and heart-healthy nuts, such as almonds
- load up on fiber—key for binding to excess cholesterol (before absorption into your system) and escorting it out of the body
- consume high-quality omega-3-rich fish oils
- ensure you eat foods high in plant sterols—organic molecules shown to deter cholesterol absorption—such as nuts, and low-gluten whole grains
- fill your diet with free-radical-busting antioxidants, such as kale and blueberries
- exercise—exercising has been found to help optimize your good:bad cholesterol ratio
- get plenty of safe sun exposure to fuel your body's production of vitamin D. Vitamin D has been shown to inhibit arterial plaque, offsetting cholesterol's impact

Protein

Protein is a macro-nutrient composed of molecules called amino acids. There are twenty-one amino acids in total. Nine of these amino acids are considered 'essential', meaning we need to obtain them from our food, as the body cannot produce them.

Proteins are the building blocks for muscles and perform a number of functions within the body. There are several different protein sources. Meat is the most commonly known food with a direct association to protein. It is a complete protein source, in that its protein has all the essential amino acids. Most other food has protein as a constituent, but most likely not a complete protein. That is why it is critical for vegetarians and vegans to understand what food combinations will deliver all the amino acids necessary for vibrant health, such as combining beans with grains. Alone they lack certain amino acids, but together they represent a complete protein source.

Fiber

Fiber is a crucial part of our diet, which explains the fiber claims draped on our boxes of cereal and loaves of bread. What's amazing about fiber is that—depending on the type of fiber—you may absorb very little, or none at all. Hence, one of the reasons why it's so important. There is no significant calorie intake, yet it provides a vital function in the body. Fiber is classified as either insoluble or soluble. Insoluble fiber, such as the fibrous material in celery, acts as a broom, helping to clean out the intestines, while soluble fiber (e.g., chia or flax seeds) behaves like a sponge, attracting and absorbing nasty toxins that find their way into the body. It can also aid in the prevention of certain cancers, hemorrhoids, and diverticulosis (a disorder which creates cramps and tenderness in the colon). Several correlations can be made regarding the incidence of disease and fiber intake. However, one thing is clear, a diet high in dietary fiber is a fundamental component of disease prevention.

Hormones... The Body's Chemical Messengers

As the title suggests, hormones are the chemical messengers of information throughout the body. They are critical to ensuring that your body functions as advertised. Any significant disruption in hormonal balance can wreak havoc on the body. Hormones play roles in everything we do, from telling us when we're hungry or feeling happy, to reproduction. Understanding how certain hormones work in our bodies is crucial in grasping the effects of foods, stress, and exercise on our bodies.

Ghrelin/Leptin/Adiponectin/Peptide YY

Ghrelin is a hormone secreted by the stomach. It sounds the alarm that we need to eat, and signals when we require more energy. Conversely, leptin, adiponectin, and peptide YY all play a part in letting us know we're full.

Leptin—secreted by fatty tissue—gives us the heads up when we are full and keeps an eye on energy stores; without it, we would lose control of our appetite. Adiponectin and peptide YY both sound the alarm, letting us know when we need to stop eating. Peptide YY (PYY) does this through increasing leptin sensitivity. Note that both proteins and fats prompt a significant release of PYY, whereas carbohydrates have a muted effect. This partially explains why we often overeat when carbs dominate our diets.

Insulin/Glucagon

Our pancreas produces insulin, (probably) the most well-known hormone. Insulin's primary function is to control our blood-sugar levels. Liken insulin to the automobile needed to drive glucose (i.e., sugar) into our cells. The pancreas goes into insulin-producing overdrive if we binge on simple carbohydrates, as our body processes these sugars very quickly.

Glucagon, on the other hand, pulls energy out of your cells, especially the liver. Low blood sugar stimulates the release of glucagon. Simplified, insulin drives glucose into the cell, and glucagon pulls it out when needed.

Cortisol

Better known as the stress hormone, cortisol—a key anti-inflammatory—is responsible for several reactions in the human body. It suppresses immune system 'over'response (i.e., an overreaction by the immune system), raises blood pressure, and decreases insulin sensitivity. Cortisol can be brought on by external factors, including lack of sleep, and stress. As you probably figured out, too much cortisol can be extremely detrimental to good health. It truly is the *Goldilocks* of hormones—it needs to be just right.

Insulin-Like Growth Factor—1

Insulin-Like Growth Factor (IGF-1) is a big player in physical recovery. Pretty much everything affects IGF-1's release in the body. Yet, excessive IGF-1 can accelerate aging, and has been linked to cancer[6].

Admittedly, this hormone review was a simplified explanation, however, for the purpose of this book, it is all that's required.

Now It's Feeding Time!

"Digestion, of all bodily functions, is the one which exercises the greatest influence on the mental state of an individual."
— Anthelme Brillat-Savarin, 18th century French writer

Hunger and Satiety

I have a tendency to be critical of overconsumption. In a world plagued with poverty, it's appalling that one of Western society's biggest problems is that we can't control our appetites.

You may have deep-rooted reasons why you rely on food. I'm not here to judge anyone's motives. I'm simply bringing attention to a generation of people obsessed with excess, in every sense of the word.

Now that you have a sense of the critical roles certain hormones play in your body, let's dig deeper into how they manage your appetite. It all starts with your hypothalamus, which houses the chemicals for hunger (i.e., Neuropeptide Y or NPY) and satiety (i.e., Cocaine and Amphetamine Regulated Transcript or CART).

The stomach releases the hormone ghrelin, which gives the signal for you to eat by stimulating NPY. Fatty tissues secrete the hormone leptin, which stimulates your satiety center (CART) to let you know when you should stop.

Things start to fall apart when these hormones stop functioning properly. When people put on weight and consistently overeat, the body becomes increasingly resistant to leptin. If the brain isn't responding to the signal of feeling full, you'll (potentially) continue eating—leading to a vicious cycle of overconsumption. Exacerbating things even further, several foods, such as high-fructose corn syrup and other simple carbohydrates, do not prompt equivalent chemical responses of satiety, thus delaying that 'full' feeling. Sticking to diets with a variety of healthy fats, protein, and whole grains will ensure that these signals are effectively delivered to your brain.

Now that we know why you feel hungry and full, let's look at what happens to the food you do eat.

Digestion

Mechanical Digestion... Chewing

We often underestimate how important chewing is to our overall nutrition.

Due to our hectic lifestyles, we pile more and more food down our throats and probably chew less than ever before. This is a big mistake because chewing stimulates the digestive system to release the appropriate juices—enzymes—it needs to begin chemically and mechanically breaking down the food. This enables the enzymes, and chemicals (later in the digestive process), to break down what we eat. If food isn't properly broken down, we will not effectively absorb all the nutrients our body needs. In this step of the digestion process, proteins are physically broken down into smaller chunks, the starch component of the carbohydrates, and fats, are physically, and chemically (albeit marginally) altered, and fibers remain intact.

The Journey Continues... The Stomach

The stomach represents a staging area for food before it enters the intestines. Acids and enzymes, such as protein-digesting pepsin, begin digesting your food before it travels to the small intestines. Cells that line the stomach detect food and start sending leptin to the brain to signal that food has arrived, decreasing appetite, and increasing metabolism. Fatty tissue in the small intestines will intensify the secretion of leptin. Along with leptin, the stomach releases cholecystokinin (CCK) to initiate downstream digestion.

> ### *Ikkuma* INFO: WATER AND MEALS
> Proper hydration is key for maintaining good health, and promoting detoxification. Yet, drinking at the wrong times can be a detriment to food digestion. When you drink water too close to eating, or during a meal, you dilute digestive enzymes and the hydrochloric acid in your stomach. Hydrochloric acid is crucial for the destruction of harmful bacteria, and allows the stomach perform its primary function: staging food for the small intestine. For optimal digestion, aim to avoid water 30-minutes before and 60-minutes after eating.

Intestines

The first stop on our intestinal-tract journey is the small intestine. Around the time nutrients enter circulation via the small intestine, the hormone peptide YY is released—signalling that we should slow down our eating by increasing leptin sensitivity. As mentioned earlier, protein and fat help release significant amounts of PYY. Carbohydrates trail far behind.

Enzymes required for digestion need a relatively hospitable environment. The small intestine is an alkaline environment (this is a good thing), which allows for these enzymes to get busy. With help from the pancreas, in the form of pancreatic enzymes, and the gall bladder in the form of bile salts, this is where nutrients are predominantly absorbed. Complex proteins are broken down into single amino acids, while complex carbohydrates are broken down into monosaccharides (i.e., glucose or fructose—sugar). In this state, both get absorbed and enter the bloodstream on the way to the liver.

Fats are more complicated. Bile salts deal with fats, which eventually pass through the intestinal wall. From here, and with the help of unique proteins, fats make their way to the liver, with a few stops along the way.

Liver

In a normal feeding state, broken-down proteins (i.e., amino acids) are either used by the liver, converted to other amino acids, converted to sugar, or leave the liver unused. If not used by the liver they are used for dozens of bodily functions, such as muscle synthesis. In times of need, amino acids stored in muscles and other tissues can be used to produce glucose, powering the body.

Carbs tell a very different story. When glucose enters the bloodstream post-absorption, the pancreas releases insulin into the bloodstream. The insulin acts as a vehicle, first transporting the sugars to the liver, producing glycogen. Glycogen is energy stored in your liver and tissues for times of need. The brain and other tissues then use whatever glucose remains as an energy source if needed.

Fructose is a unique carbohydrate, in that, it is primarily the liver that can use fructose directly. In the liver—under normal circumstances—fructose is converted to glucose and, as explained earlier, predominantly stored as glycogen.

Lastly, fats simply get transported around the body in the form of fatty acids, performing key cellular functions, and stored to use as future fuel.

Two primary conditions change the dynamics of how the liver and body deal with proteins, carbs, and fat: a state of fasting, and a state of overconsumption. In a state of extended fasting, the liver tends to convert amino acids to glucose—sacrificing muscle development—and stores it as glycogen to help maintain blood sugar levels.

Carbs get hogged by the liver and saved for optimal brain function, and maintaining blood sugar levels. Depending on the severity and duration of the fast, fats get used as fuel through a process called ketosis. Major organs can operate well using ketones for fuel, which helps to reduce the blow to our glycogen stores and muscles.

In a state of overconsumption, which seemingly represents 2/3 of the North American population (the approximate proportion of people overweight), things get complicated.

Proteins do not pose a huge problem. Remember what I said earlier? Protein, through the body's release of PYY, sends a strong signal to the brain that we should stop eating. However, in the case of excess protein consumption, the surplus amino acids are converted to glucose—immediately used for energy, stored as glycogen, or converted to fat.

Here comes the ugly part—carbs. Put quite simply, once the liver and muscles cannot store any more glucose in the form of glycogen, excess carbs get converted into fatty acids (palmitic acid) and dropped off throughout the body for fuel, creating loads of fatty tissue.

The greater problem lies in the reaction this fat has with the brain. Constant overconsumption begins to dampen the brain's sensitivity to leptin (i.e., the hormone that helps you feel full). Without feeling full, we tend to overeat, and the vicious cycle begins. All this excess glucose elevates insulin in your bloodstream and will, over time, decrease the liver's insulin sensitivity, and reduce overall cell sensitivity to insulin.

In effect, your cells become insulin resistant, requiring more and more insulin to deliver glucose into your cells. In this state, blood sugar is now getting out of control. Elevated blood sugar starts to create nicks in your arteries—much like sand in a hose—paving the way for an inflammatory response. This inflammatory response is the manifestation of your body damage control.

As we continue down the rabbit hole, this potential state of insulin resistance starts to trick the body into thinking that it has low blood sugar. You can liken this to a chronic pain you've had for a while. When you begin to experience the pain you are very conscious of it, however, after a while, you may become used to it. In this situation, the body gets used to this elevated state of insulin resistance, and it becomes the new status quo. Weeds and insects that develop a resistance to a new herbicide or pesticide, provide another great analogy. Eventually, as the weeds and insects develop greater resistance, more and more herbicide or pesticide is required. Similarly, in a state of overconsumption, the body is conditioned into thinking it needs more and more insulin. Our bodies are no longer giving us the proper signals needed to effectively manage our appetites.

Cortisol production is our body's next response. Amazingly, despite the saturation of glucose in the body, the body's insulin resistance prompts the production of cortisol, which will work to convert tissue in the body, such as muscle, to glucose. Since muscle is used to store glucose in the first place, the muscle decay amplifies the problem. A good portion of the excess glucose eventually gets converted into fat and is mainly deposited around the abdomen. This abdominal fat is not inert, as it secretes hormones and molecules that promote harmful inflammation. Moreover, this fat buildup begins to shuttle fatty acids to the organs it surrounds, such as the liver, potentially resulting in conditions such as non-alcoholic fatty-liver disease.

Left unchecked, overconsumption can lead to insulin resistance so severe that a person may develop Type-II Diabetes—a metabolic condition of chronic insulin resistance, characterized by elevated blood sugar.

The last destructive process in this chain reaction is the production of advanced glycation end products (AGEs). AGEs are formed when all that excess sugar floating around starts to react with proteins in the body, and oxidizes. They pose an enormous risk due to the mess they make in your body, as they further damage the insulin and leptin receptors (worsening the risk of diabetes), and, due to the DNA damage they cause, may accelerate aging.

I Have a 'Gut' Feeling

> *"It is a hard matter, my fellow citizens, to argue with the belly, since it has no ears."*
> —PLUTARCH, 1ST CENTURY PHILOSOPHER

"Vibrant Intestinal Flora"—"The joyful convolutions of life allow us to digest and benefit from the world's abundance."—Sheila LeBlanc

You've heard the expressions, 'butterflies in your stomach' and 'gut-wrenching'. There's a reason why our emotions often manifest in our gastrointestinal tract, or gut.

We effectively have two brains, one in your skull and one in our gut. Both are created from the same tissue at fetal development; one develops into the central nervous system (in the brain, with 80-100 billion neurons), with the other becoming your enteric nervous system (in the gut, boasting over 100 million neurons). The vagus nerve helps these two systems communicate. Therefore, it makes perfect sense that our gut health will have a profound effect on our psychological health. Surprising to many, the gut produces approximately 90% of our serotonin (i.e., happiness hormone). So, a happy gut means a happy camper. Our gut is truly the holy grail when it comes to our overall health and happiness. Nurture our gut, and our body will thank us for it.

There are trillions of cells in our body, yet, oddly enough, over 90% of the genetic material in our body—not *our* genetic material by the way—is found in the gut in the form of fungi, bacteria (both good and bad), and microflora. This under-appreciated and rarely-understood part of our physiology influences our moods, is our portal for getting healthy nutrients to our organs, and represents the majority of our immune system. The gut is our body's first line of defense. It is estimated that our gut is responsible for up to 80% of our immune system, so once our gut is compromised, all bodily functions, and thus overall health, may be compromised as a result. Unfortunately, few people realize the crucial importance of their gut, as it relates to the functioning of the immune system.

What Is Compromising Our Gut Health?

The following have been shown to destroy our gut flora:

- *Genetically engineered foods* typically contain higher levels of toxins, which can wreak havoc on gut flora. I'll get into the Genetically Modified Organism (GMO) discussion shortly. If, after that, you aren't completely disturbed by our existing food supply-chain, then I have been unsuccessful in effectively laying out the facts.
- *Sucralose* has been shown to destroy upwards of 50% of our beneficial bacteria, and affects the efficacy of our digestive enzymes[7]. I really do think the motto of the 1970s and 80s was how much crap can we invent to trick the public into eating more crap. Just in case you missed my point, sucralose = crap. It shouldn't go near your mouth, let alone in it.
- *Processed foods* contain little to no beneficial bacteria, and their typically high level of sugars creates a favorable environment for pathogenic anaerobic bacteria to thrive, thus suppressing good bacteria. These pathogenic microbes damage the integrity of our gut wall. Once the good bacteria have been compromised,

toxins and "bad" bacteria may more easily enter the bloodstream, potentially increasing the risk of developing a host of conditions, including allergies, and ADHD.
- *Antibiotics* deserve a lot of attention. While there are many different types, all antibiotics kill good and bad bacteria. While killing the infections they're meant to attack, antibiotics can also destroy beneficial bacteria in our gut. And I'm not just talking about what doctors prescribe for infection, as most people are ingesting antibiotics in their food without even realizing it. Caged Animal Feed Operations (CAFOs)—now a conventional method for raising livestock—routinely use antibiotics to ostensibly keep the cows, chickens, and pigs alive. Antibiotics are also instrumental in helping animals grow bigger in a shorter time.

The U.S. FDA reported that factory farms used over 29 million pounds of antibiotics in 2009. It is estimated that over 80% of all antibiotics used in the U.S. are utilized for some agricultural purpose. But wait, it gets worse. Manure from these operations is awash with antibiotics, contaminating the crops for which it provides nutrients. Eventually, antibiotics make their way to our stomachs, and so the damage begins. Our reliance on fast-food has turned food into a manufacturing business instead of an agricultural one. Yet we have evolved?

When you neglect gut health, the good bacteria (approximately 85% of all bacteria in your gut) is compromised, and yeast can grow unabated; creating holes in your intestinal lining, known as 'leaky gut syndrome.' This can cause a host of problems, such as providing pathogens and other food particles a clear path into the bloodstream. Once invaders get past this first line of defense, they are often recognized as pathogenic, instigating an immune response. This response comes with it a variety of potential complications, namely, allergies and autoimmune disorders.

> **_Ikkuma_ INFO: KNOW YOUR ANTIBIOTICS**
>
> The New England Journal of Medicine found that within the first five days of taking azithromycin, a common antibiotic used to treat ailments like ear infections and bronchitis, your chances of dying from heart failure increases by 250%, as compared to taking amoxicillin, another common antibiotic. Know the medicine you are taking. We often don't take responsibility for what we put into our bodies. For the few times you need medicine, it wouldn't hurt to perform some due diligence.

Protecting and Repairing Your Gut

Let's look at how you can protect your gut. Hopefully, after learning about your gut, you should now realize how critical this part of your physiology is to overall health.

Here is a quick list of what you can do to keep your gut functioning well:

- avoid the good-bacteria-killing culprits previously listed, with a caveat that antibiotics—medication designed to kill bacteria—should only be taken when entirely necessary. The problem lies with these antibiotics being broad-spectrum (i.e., non-specific, they kill both good and bad bacteria). Good bacteria need to be nourished, not destroyed. Since the non-medical use of antibiotics is not allowed in organic farming, ensure you eat organically raised animals. For beef, look for 'grass-finished free-range', and for chickens try to find 'pastured' sources
- nourishing your gut flora with fermented foods and probiotics is crucial for proper brain function, key to regulating your moods. Whole fermented food sources, such as sauerkraut and kimchi, are excellent choices. Organic yogurt, preferably non-dairy, is another good source of beneficial bacteria
- control your stress. Later on, I'll give you some tips on how to do that, but know that if you don't control stress, your gut health will be one of the many negative consequences. Stress has been shown to increase the permeability of our gut, and be detrimental to our sensitive microflora[8].

Part TWO
Disease... Know Thy Enemy

"What can't be cured must be endured."
—ENGLISH PROVERB

We are in the middle of an obesity pandemic. To most people, obesity is to blame for the skyrocketing incidences of disease in the Western world. This is painfully ironic considering that in, the same breath we claim to be the earth's most advanced society. Like clockwork (across the world), as our wealth grows so too does our consumption of packaged and fast foods. And consume we do.

The average U.S. citizen's calorie consumption has risen from 2200 to over 2700 in the past 20 years. We are devolving into a society that is plagued with preventable diseases. Not only are we over-consuming, but what we are eating is often destructive to our bodies. Our typical response to this path of destruction left by our poor eating decisions is to mask the symptoms with drugs, which (as mentioned) often create more havoc.

The best way to manage disease is not to cure it, but to prevent it from occurring in the first place. To do this, we need to create an environment in our body that is conducive to vibrant health. We need to focus on prevention. Don't worry about having a special diet for cancer, and another for diabetes. We need to be smart with all our decisions. Forget fad diets and gimmicky get-thin-fast swindles. Being disease-free isn't about shortcuts. Being disease-free is about making smart, informed decisions day-in-day-out. And most of these smart decisions are easy. Yet, our godlike devotion to the Western diet makes dumb decisions a lot more palatable than smart ones.

Alas, all is not lost. I believe that once you are faced with the reality of your statistical future, you'll want to change.

Key Precursors to Disease

Before we dive into some common diseases, their impacts, and tips on prevention, let's look at two commonly discussed topics often linked to disease: obesity and chronic inflammation.

i. Obesity

> *"My doctor told me to stop having intimate dinners for four. Unless there are three other people."*
> —ORSON WELLES, AMERICAN ACTOR

I admit that I used to be a 'fat'ist. I'm not proud of it, but yes, I harshly judged people based on their size. This wasn't because I looked down on them. It was quite the opposite. I just didn't know how people could squander such a beautiful gift as their health. I have since taken a more empathetic approach and see it as a challenge to help people break the cycle of obesity, regardless of why they ended up obese in the first place.

We've all read studies highlighting the high percentages of the population who are overweight and obese. What does this mean? Remember, overweight refers to having a Body Mass Index (BMI) of 25 or above, while obese refers to a BMI over 30. Out of context, these numbers don't tell us anything. Nonetheless, try checking your BMI (there are several tables online to help you with the calculation). If you find you are above 25, then take it as a wake-up call. There is one small caveat. If you are very athletic and highly muscular, this measurement is not relevant, and you likely don't even need to be checking your BMI in the first place.

It is estimated that two-thirds of North Americans are overweight, and over one-third are obese. As reported in the USA Today, if present trends continue, obesity will cost Americans approximately $344 billion in medical-related expenses by 2018[1]. What's even more disturbing is that over 15% of American children are overweight with another 15% at risk of becoming overweight. Consequently, we are seeing skyrocketing rates of Type-II Diabetes in children.

This is one of those, "Are you fucking kidding me?", moments. How the hell can our children even become an obesity statistic? How can we, as adults, look in the mirror and be ok with this? This isn't about loving yourself regardless of your body type. I see this argument all the time. People are encouraged to accept themselves the way they are. Of course, we should never be ashamed of our appearance, but this is not about self-esteem. This is about the survival of our children. Stop making this a vanity discussion, because it's not. It's a health issue. Childhood obesity is not healthy. It's a road to disease, and as adults, we should be mortified at the existence of the mere existence of a childhood obesity statistic.

When discussing obesity, there are two major types of fat we often refer to: visceral fat (i.e., fat that is around your midsection and surrounds your organs), and subcutaneous fat (i.e., just under the skin). Once you have a fat cell, unless you undergo liposuction, you essentially have it for life. It may contract and expand, but it will, for all intents and purposes, always be there. It is particularly critical to encourage our youth to adopt healthy habits as early as possible, since most fat cells are created by the time we hit puberty.

It's hard to pinpoint the specific cause of an individual's belly fat. Regardless of the reason why you find yourself battling the bulge, visceral fat is a clear sign that you need to refocus your health regimen. Due to its proximity to your organs, this type of fat is considered the most dangerous. To reduce this 'belly' fat, your diet should be the primary focus, with sleep, stress, and exercise not far behind. While it may not be news to many people, I feel it is important to keep in mind that, to successfully combat obesity, we need to attack it from every angle.

Although narrowing down the specific causes for putting on excess fat is tricky at best, cortisol and elevated blood sugar are the most probable culprits in some capacity. Cortisol (the stress hormone), one of the main hormones associated with obesity and the related negative processes leading to it, is released at the end of the dreaded insulin resistance cycle. We need cortisol to survive, but in excess, it eats away at muscle and adds to your visceral (abdominal) fat.

There are several things you can do to keep cortisol from spiking:

- manage stress in all aspects of your life. Stress can create chronically high levels of cortisol in the body

- get adequate sleep. Later on I will outline effective ways to optimize your sleep
- avoid excessive sugar and keep blood sugar levels balanced. Sugar comes in many disguises. Don't be fooled. I will drill this home repeatedly
- exercise with a purpose. Moderate exercise does wonders to manage cortisol levels

Elevated blood sugar comes from many different sources. However, the process creating this situation is common regardless of the cause. Simply put, eating highly-processed and refined carbohydrates will spike your blood sugar. Quantity is a factor but these foods should be avoided altogether.

Here are some surefire tips to help control your blood sugar intake:

- eat smaller meals
- fat, fiber and protein contribute to regulating the absorption of sugar into the blood, helping stabilize your blood sugar, and give you more of that 'full' feeling
- reduce refined and simple carbohydrate consumption. This includes high-fructose corn syrup (present in many processed foods), general sugars, and overly processed grains, such as those you'll find in white bread and highly refined whole-wheat products
- eat fruits in moderation—in that they contain significant amounts of fructose. They contain crucial vitamins, antioxidants, fiber, and other phytonutrients
- when possible, substitute HFCS and sugar with organic stevia or pure dextrose
- try to stick with low glycemic foods (see *Ikkuma Info: Glycemic Index*)
- don't be afraid of fats. Healthy fats such as those found in avocados and fish oil are part of a healthy lifestyle

> ### *Ikkuma* **INFO: GLYCEMIC INDEX**
> The glycemic index is a standardized method to measure how much a specific food will increase your blood sugar. The scale is from zero to one hundred. Use the following guidelines to ensure you stick to lower glycemic foods as much as possible:
> - High Glycemic Foods (greater than 70) — glucose, corn flakes, white bread, candy, popcorn, baked potatoes, white bagels, instant oatmeal, soda crackers, watermelons
> - Moderate Glycemic Foods (56–69) — oatmeal, white rice, whole wheat products, raisins, sugar, sweet potatoes, corn on the cob, ice cream, spaghetti, honey
> - Low Glycemic Foods (55 or less) — most fruits and vegetables, whole grain products, brown rice, chicken, meat, eggs, fish, nuts, beans, milk

Many vegetarians contend that they have a much lower chance of becoming obese than carnivores. They support these claims with anecdotal accounts of how slim vegetarians and vegans are, relative to meat eaters. These generalized claims and statements are misplaced, in that being a meat eater means a lot of different things to different people. Eating processed meats and excess red meat, versus eating meat in moderation, are two very different profiles. We need to be careful before placing labels on meat eaters or vegetarians alike.

I'm not judging vegetarians or vegans. Each to his or her own. Although I'm not a vegan or vegetarian, I do agree that we eat way too much meat. A healthy diet, complete with a variety of whole foods (e.g., vegetables and fruit), avoiding refined carbohydrates, and incorporating meat in moderation, is a recipe for avoiding obesity.

Those reading this who are overweight or obese should not lose hope and submit to the idea that whatever they lose will be gained back. Gaining weight after you lose it is the result of a yo-yo diet. Life isn't about diets. Life and health are about balance. Find your balance. It might not be easy at first, but your body will adjust, as it did to your obesity.

Creating a foundation of good health will help ensure that those pounds stay off. Start today, and you'll reap the benefits of weight loss almost immediately. Even minor weight loss can have dramatic effects on your risk of developing chronic diseases. In one study amongst a group of breast cancer survivors, a relatively small 3kg weight loss decreased their risk of recurrence by 24%[2].

Even something as simple as curbing your calorie intake for only 48 hours has been shown to reduce fat in the liver by up to 25%. We all need to start somewhere. Set manageable goals, and remember that every pound of weight loss counts. A combination of the diet and fitness recommendations in this book can help you begin to eat away at excess body weight almost immediately (see *Ikkuma Info: Intermittent Fasting*).

The key is to take two steps forward for every step back. I know it's not easy. I've tried tirelessly to help those close to me, but in the end, we all need to find our own motivation.

> *Ikkuma* **INFO: INTERMITTENT FASTING**
>
> One method some people use to burn fat is intermittent fasting. This could involve an occasional 14–16 hour fast. For instance, on a Wednesday night, have dinner at around 7 pm where instead of eating breakfast on Thursday morning you simply drink water, adding pure lemon juice, and wait until lunch for your first meal. That would result in a fast of just over 16 hours, helping to expel toxins from your system, while increasing white blood cells[3]. Moreover, it is theorized that the glycogen stored in the liver and other muscle tissue lasts approximately 12-16 hours before it is used up (depending on activity). After burning these reserves, the body will resort to burning the most readily available fat stores. That's why eating an early dinner is key. It allows the liver to recover during your sleep, depleting glycogen. As an added benefit, when you have your morning workout you are (potentially) increasing your rate of fat burning.

ii. Chronic Inflammation

Indirectly, when discussing topics such as gut health and obesity, we have touched on many factors that can lead to what is called chronic inflammation. Inflammation is a natural series of chemical reactions in the body triggered by an abnormal stimulation. It can be caused by something biological, physical, emotional, or chemical.

One simple example of abnormal physical stimulation could be stubbing your toe. We all recognize this inflammation as normal and expected; our toe gets swollen, begins to heal, and then returns to normal.

Chronic inflammation refers to a state of systemic inflammation brought on by diet (strongly correlated to obesity), stress, pathogens, and pollutants, to name a few. It is a state where your body is constantly battling to heal itself—characterized by elevated cortisol and adrenal levels. This type of inflammation, left unaddressed, often leads to tissue destruction, and a host of diseases.

Due to its involvement in many health problems, I will refer to chronic inflammation throughout the book. However, here are a few examples of specific causes of chronic inflammation to give you an initial perspective on how it develops:

- High-Sugar Foods: excess blood sugar damages the sensitive lining of our blood vessels, prompting an immune response (i.e., inflammation) from the body. This involves using cholesterol, amongst other mechanisms, to repair the vessel lining
- Acidic Diet: a constantly acidic environment within the body damages tissue, prompting an immune response. Processed foods, refined carbohydrates, and alcohol are guilty of promoting an acidic pH in the body
- Increased Salt Intake: excess salt intake results in increased water retention in the blood. This increases blood volume, and, in turn, the pressure within the vessels. Over time, this will damage the lining of blood vessels, prompting an immune response
- Chronic Stress: excess cortisol—which, as we now know, is exacerbated by stress—contributes to the insulin resistance brought on by chronically elevated blood sugar. As seen earlier, the damage from this increased blood sugar prompts an immune response

Those are just a few common examples of how chronic inflammation is manifested. Once chronic inflammation takes hold, it can lead to several debilitating diseases such as diabetes, cardiovascular disease, cancer, and arthritis.

Let's single out cancer and walk through chronic inflammation's role in its development.

The process starts with chronic inflammation stimulating the immune system, which in turn increases the rate of cell replication. Telomeres within the cell (located at the end of chromosomes), protect them from damage during replication. Over time, as the rate of replication increases, the length of these telomeres shortens. This exposes the chromosomes to damage, resulting in premature aging and possibly, over time, cancer. This is simply one mechanism; several others come into play for a variety of diseases.

To reduce the damage (i.e., oxidative stress) caused by chronic inflammation, consumption of antioxidant-loaded fruits and vegetables is critical. Here are some other tips to reduce chronic inflammation—note that I will explain many of the suggestions in the following list throughout the book:

- eliminate sugars and reduce processed and white grain consumption, while focusing on whole, ancient grains. Following a low-glycemic index (low sugar) diet will help maintain healthy insulin levels. Note that the glycemic index, as stated earlier, is a standardized measure of how rapidly blood sugar levels rise after consuming a particular food
- practice deep breathing. This rids metabolic waste gasses through the lungs
- avoid trans fats and oxidized cholesterol. Beware of super-heated foods and oils, such as olive oil. Extra-virgin olive oil oxidizes at a lower temperature than other cooking oils, such as coconut oil
- get your sleep. Sleep helps to relax the nervous system and allows the body's tissues to recover
- ensure a proper omega balance. Ideally, the ratio of omega-6s to omega-3s should be 1:1, rather than the 15:1 ratio typical in today's Western diet[4]. Vegetable oils are a major source of omega-6s
- maintain a healthy weight. A more telling indicator is the waist-to-hip ratio. The presence of significant visceral fat is an indication of chronic inflammation
- exercise regularly. Proper exercise—from walking and restorative yoga to resistance training and sports—increases oxygenation of

tissues through increased blood flow and breathing
- optimize vitamin levels, more particularly vitamin D. The best source of vitamin D is through direct exposure to the sun's rays (in moderation). Nature knows best
- reduce stress. Stress causes hypertension, which increases blood pressure. High blood pressure damages the circulatory system. Stress also increases cortisol levels, damaging gut flora, and causing a host of other blood-sugar issues
- keep hydrated. Acidic metabolic waste that is not eliminated contributes to inflammation. Plenty of pure water helps to alkalize and flush toxins out of your system through the kidneys

Common Diseases

Now that we've set the framework regarding the scope of disease's grip on society, and the two main precursors for disease are understood, we can now examine a few of the serious diseases currently rampant in our society, and discuss some tips for preventing them. Before we dive into it, I'd like to touch on a common misconception, namely, that genetics plays a leading role in our risk of developing a significant disease.

Epigenetics

Society often uses genetics as a scapegoat for the cause of several diseases. I'm sure you've heard, "My father had colon cancer, so chances are I'll get it to." I'll show you that this isn't a cut 'n dry cause and effect relationship. Regardless of your genetics, you play the role of the conductor when it comes to allowing diseases to take hold of your body.

Stop hitching your horse to an excuse and take control. Why dwell on what you can't change? Start doing everything possible to improve what you can change instead.

The field of study related to disease and genetics is called epigenetics. Epigenetics investigates the correlation between your genetic expression and disease. One famous epigenetic study, *The Human Genome Project* (started in 1990), sought to map out all human genes, and ascertain how to cure or prevent diseases by controlling how genes express themselves.

Its initial premise was that information traveled from DNA to proteins, not vice versa. However, this is not entirely true. Scientists have determined that the environment—that is, what you think, eat, and are exposed to—effects DNA and how genes express themselves. In other words, it's two-way communication.

Genes can be activated (i.e., expressed) or deactivated (i.e., remain inert) by the environment. I liken it to having one hundred doors (genes), some are locked (no predisposition to a disease) and some aren't (predisposition to a disease). Even if a door is unlocked, unless you choose to walk through it (creating the environment), you obviously have no chance of getting to the other side. That is, the environment that your cells are exposed to, both inside and outside the body, have a considerable effect on how the cells behave. Each cell has a consciousness. Remember, communication flows in both directions.

That means your fate is not necessarily pre-determined by your genetic make-up. You have significant control over your destiny, and over which genes will play a vital role in your health. That is why I am not a big proponent of genomic testing for individuals. Learning that you have a predisposition to a certain disease or condition should not necessarily change your habits, as you should already be living the healthiest lifestyle possible. Creating a healthy environment within the body will work to protect you from all disease. Testing may create unnecessary stress, and we all know that stress can be detrimental to your health.

Nutrition has a direct effect in creating a positive environment for proper cellular function. For instance, we all have tumor suppressing genes, and we also have histones, which can effectively neutralize these genes. Cruciferous foods such as broccoli and cabbage act as histone inhibitors, thus allowing the tumor-suppressing genes to do their duty of combating cancers. The more of these foods you eat, the better chance you give yourself to prevent or defeat cancer.

A major review on cancer and diet prepared for the U.S. Congress in 1981 estimated that genetics determines less than 3% of your cancer risk[5]. This is further corroborated by a massive study in China that involved 880 million citizens. It clearly showed that cancer rates among people of similar genetic make-up were significantly different depending on where they lived. Another study by Ken Carroll from the University of Western Ontario showed a strong correlation between a person's geographic location and the diseases they developed[6]. In other words, a person's environment, not genetics, is the main driving force behind diseases such as cancer.

Genetics can no longer be the narrative for development of most diseases. You're doing yourself a disservice if you dwell on what you can't change. How you treat your body serves as a far more reliable determinant of your future than your genetic make-up. Too many people look for reasons to absolve themselves from the responsibility of managing their health; I am here to encourage you to forego the excuses—your destiny lies in your hands. Proper nutrition, limiting toxins, and positive mental health are key for encouraging your genes to act in a disease-fighting capacity.

Now, understanding that it is mainly us that control our fate, let's dive into some of the important diseases that weigh heavily on society.

Cancer

Cancer is one word you never want to hear from your doctor. It is a horrible ordeal. Simply awful. I lived this first hand with my friend Brad. His suffering was so intense that those of us who were close to him couldn't help but feel his pain at a visceral level. Cancer can be beaten but today's Western diet, and our associated bad habits, are not helping us win the fight. Depressingly, according to www.cancer.org, well over 1 in 3 Americans will be diagnosed with cancer in their lifetime. If you have had cancer or have it now, then I pray that some of the advice in this book may help you.

Our cells are constantly in the cycle of growth (i.e., replication), repair, and death. When a cell replicates (i.e., mitosis) there is always the opportunity for there to be errors in replication. The more often cell replicates, the more chance for error. Our bodies attempt to control these errors through a healthy immune system.

When there are too many abnormal or mutated cells, and you lose the ability to destroy them at the necessary rate, you develop cancer. That is, your immune system is unable to ebb the flow of uncontrolled replication of abnormal cells.

Chronic inflammation can promote this environment of increased cell replication in a body with a compromised defense system. Via several hormonal responses, chronic inflammation increases the growth rate of tissues and compromises apoptosis (i.e., the process of programmed cell death). If chronic inflammation does not create full blown cancer, as explained earlier, it is still a potential cause of several other degenerative diseases.

Later in the book, we will discuss toxins and the several chemicals that have been shown to increase cancer rates in mammals (i.e., carcinogens). Some you may know very well, such as nitrites (a preservative found in most hot dogs and other processed meats), aflatoxins (found on moldy corn and peanuts), and some artificial sweeteners.

Let's dig a little deeper into the mechanism behind the journey of a healthy cell becoming cancerous. Cancer has three general phases: mutation, promotion, and progression.

- *Mutation:* most toxins or carcinogens cannot cause cancer on their own. They need to be metabolized (converted) by enzymes in the cell. This new byproduct (i.e. an adduct), then attacks the DNA. If your body doesn't repair the DNA before the cell replicates, you get newly formed mutated daughter cells (i.e., cancer cells). Once this becomes uncontrollable within the body, it is difficult to reverse
- *Promotion:* this phase offers a little more hope. Picture the mutation phase as the beginning of a viral video; without other factors to help the video spread throughout the digital world, it would just die an unimpressive death. Cancer behaves similarly. The promotion phase is where your key influencers help spread the material and allow it to grow unabated. In this phase, we start to control our destiny, because, without the proper conditions in which it proliferates—such as an acidic environment—cancer cannot overtake the body
- *Progression:* once cancer has metastasized—transferred to another non-adjacent organ or part of the body—we are in real trouble. Imagine weeds coming up through the lawn, and then somehow popping up in your driveway as well. Cancer has spread and has

become difficult to contain

Some studies have shown that reducing the number of particular proteins in your diet decreases the enzyme activity necessary for binding carcinogens to DNA. The present recommended daily allowance (RDA) for protein is about 10% of our food intake. Most Americans on average consume upwards of 15% of their daily food intake in protein. Some animal studies suggest that this alone, depending on the type of protein, puts us at greater risk of getting cancer[7].

With that said, further animal studies support the theory that it's not solely the amount of protein, but the types of protein that are relevant. One study in question, analyzing experiments performed on rats, showed that plant-based proteins did not promote cancer growth at levels of 20% protein, where casein protein—found in dairy milk—did[8]. Later, I will investigate the challenges with dairy.

Common Cancers

i. Breast

The risk of getting breast cancer correlates with excessive exposure to estrogen and progesterone. This excessive exposure is typically observed in women who reach puberty at a younger age and reach menopause later in life.

Studies show that women are indeed maturing earlier compared to 10-30 years ago[9]. Relative to rural Chinese women, women in the Western world are exposed to over 2.5 times the levels of estrogen[10].

There are many different theories attempting to explain this extension of womens' reproductive lives. As will be explored in further detail later in the book, exposure to many common toxins and chemicals, namely xenoestrogens like phthalates—found in plastics and other household chemicals—disrupt the proper functioning of hormones. Another theory blames our Western diet—high in animal protein and refined carbohydrates—for this excessive hormone exposure.

I mention 'excuses' a lot. The general public loves excuses because having an excuse absolves us from the responsibility to proactively influence our fate. Many people blame genetics as the primary cause of developing breast cancer, and while I won't dispute the fact that genetics does play a role, it's important to qualify genetic's actual impact.

For instance, one study attributes less than 3% of breast cancer cases to genetics[11]. Even if genetics were to account for two to three times this number, it would still hold true to say that family history predetermines a relatively small percentage of breast cancer cases. We need to focus on controlling our environment if we want to combat this disease. Put the odds in your favor. Control what goes in your body, control what goes on your body, and control how you keep your body conditioned.

ii. Prostate and Colon

Rates of colorectal cancer vary considerably from one country to another, with Western societies having the highest incidence of the disease. Many experts in the field argue that our environment is a primary contributing factor to this disease. One report by the World Cancer Research Fund found that rates of colorectal cancer in high-income countries are four times higher than in medium to low-income countries[12]. Many countries that have grown wealthier have seen rates of the disease double since the 1970s[13]. It is clear that lifestyle, environment, and diet—not genetics—are the main contributors to developing colorectal disease.

Knowing that diet plays a key role in creating that inhospitable environment for colorectal cancer to thrive begs the question, what needs to be fixed? Increasing fiber intake and consuming meat in moderation reduces the risk of developing colorectal cancer. One study's findings showed a reduced risk of nearly 50% when considering these dietary guidelines[14]. To clarify, by fiber I'm talking about natural occurring fiber in fruits, vegetables, and whole grains—not the fiber found in supplements or fortified food products.

Prostate cancer inflicts over 25% of American males[15]. While I recommend the same dietary guidelines as above, I will also stress the importance of removing dairy from your diet. Some studies posit that increased dairy intake doubles the risk of developing prostate cancer[16].

Managing your environment, diet, and lifestyle is imperative to reducing your cancer risk. Cancer is not a natural condition. Some societies and cultures that still eat a predominantly plant-based diet, and live relatively free of environmental toxins, have low incidences of cancer. In the Western world, we continue to rely on modern medicine to combat the disease, instead maintaining a healthy lifestyle. Evolving from a processed diet to one filled with the phytonutrients (i.e., plant nutrients), and antioxidants found in whole foods will help keep you cancer-free.

Diabetes

Diabetes—specifically Type-II Diabetes (Mellitus)—wins the award for the trendiest disease in North America. Over 8% of Americans have diabetes, and nearly one-third of them don't even know it. Our tendency to overeat, and our heavy reliance on processed and fast food, will further fuel this alarming trend.

Before we get into the different types of diabetes, let's quickly review what we have already learned about our metabolism:

- after we have eaten a meal, through a series of reactions in the digestive process, carbohydrates are broken down into simple sugars (glucose)
- the pancreas produces insulin, which is critical for getting glucose to our muscles, and other cells that need it
- the glucose gets used for immediate energy, stored as glycogen (for energy in the future), or metabolized and stored it as fat

Type-I Diabetes is an autoimmune disease where the body's immune system mistakenly attacks healthy insulin-producing beta cells of the pancreas. This renders the pancreas incapable of producing insulin. While commonly believed to be genetic, or simply luck of the draw, this is not necessarily the case. Although a genetic predisposition is a factor, studies have shown that a baby's environment could be a significant contributor to the development of this disease. For instance, the introduction of cow's milk to a baby's diet has been linked to the development of Type-I Diabetes[17]. There are also studies showing the correlation between a country's per capita dairy consumption and the incidence of Type-I Diabetes[18]. The stats are even more startling for genetically susceptible children.

The China Study by Campbell and Campbell[19] explains the process they believe is the basis for this phenomenon:

- the baby is fed cow's milk at an early age
- the milk makes its way to the baby's small intestine where the protein is broken down into the individual amino acids
- some babies are not able to fully digest the cow's milk. In such cases, some of these amino acid fragments can find their way into the infant's bloodstream and can be recognized as invaders by their immune system
- the immune system goes about its work destroying these invaders. However, some of the protein fragments look similar to healthy pancreatic cells (i.e., beta cells) responsible for producing insulin
- if the body loses the ability to distinguish between these fragments and healthy pancreatic cells, the infant's body destroys the pancreatic cells, leaving the baby with Type-I Diabetes for life

You can make your own conclusions. It does seem logical that we should not feed our infants something that is inherently difficult to digest. We have evolved over thousands of years, and are designed to nurse our young. If doing otherwise puts our children at risk, why would we take the chance?

Type-II Diabetes is an entirely different animal. Even though the pancreas is still able to produce insulin, the body no longer responds to it—it has developed a resistance. In other words, your cells—which require insulin to deliver them glucose—are so saturated with fats and lipids, that insulin can no longer perform its job. The insulin receptors of a cell are desensitized to insulin. Therefore, with the insulin rendered ineffective, the body can no longer metabolize sugars and control blood sugar levels. Liken it to heading to your favorite restaurant, which you have been eating at for years, but because they let in so many tourists, you're now turned away.

The effects of developing diabetes go well beyond the daily routine of measuring blood sugar levels and taking insulin shots. Diabetes is a disease that opens the door to several other serious complications.

Here are just a few related risks, according to the Centers For Disease Control and Prevention[20]:

- 2–4 times the risk of getting a stroke
- 2–4 times the risk of heart disease
- leading cause of blindness in adults
- leading cause of end-stage kidney disease

Once again, the key to dealing with disease is to prevent it from developing. Diabetes is no different. You will recognize many of the following tips to avoid developing diabetes, in that they make up a typical 'To-Do' list to combat many Western Diseases:

- follow a low-glycemic-index diet
- consume 7–10 servings of vegetables and fruit per day; this will help to alkalize the body, helping prevent inflammation
- consume plenty of fiber-rich foods, such as beans and legumes, as they help to reduce cholesterol and maintain healthy elimination of toxins
- exercise daily
- maintain a healthy body weight
- manage stress levels. This will reduce cortisol levels and prevent insulin resistance

The sad reality is that Type-II Diabetes is, for the most part, preventable if you adopt a healthy regimen. Therein lies the irony; the one disease we have direct control over is the one that poses the greatest present risk to society. Diabetes may well be the trophy for the generation that over-consumes. Unfortunately, this trophy has a less than flattering inscription, "To a society that ate itself to death...". I may sound alarmist, but when we look back in 20 years, we'll be asking ourselves why we didn't wake up when we still had the time.

Cardiovascular Disease and Stroke

Here are some startling facts: nearly 40% of Americans will die from some form of heart or circulatory failure, with women 8x more likely to die from heart disease than from breast cancer[21].

Though the death rate for people developing heart disease has decreased significantly since the 1970s, the actual incidence of occurrence is nearly identical[22]. This trend has little, if anything, to do with an improvement in our quality of life. Instead, it is almost entirely due to advances in medical treatment, including the nearly-routine heart bypass surgery. This procedure is a pharmaceutical company's dream, as patients become dependent on drugs for a prolonged period following surgery.

As I explained earlier, your absolute cholesterol has less to say about your risk of heart disease than your HDL (i.e., good cholesterol) to LDL cholesterol (i.e., potentially bad cholesterol) ratio. When the endothelial cells lining your arterial walls get damaged—from a poor diet, for example—small and dense LDL particles get stuck and cause inflammation. When this kind of damage occurs, the immune response causes scarring, damage to the blood vessels, and plaque (i.e., fatty and greasy deposits) build-up. It is this build-up that restricts flow through the vessels, thus reducing the flow of blood to our vital organs—the beginning of heart disease. From here it can very quickly escalate to a critical level—blockage of the artery. Subsequently, the muscles in the heart are starved of the oxygen they need to function. Muscle cells eventually die, kicking off the severe pain and complications of a heart attack. Keeping inflammation at bay is key to reducing the risk of cardiovascular disease.

Section TWO

Part ONE
Foods To 'Live' By

(Ikkuma Translation: Feeding The Fire)

"Nourishment"—"The nourishment that sustains us comes in many places and in many forms."—Sheila LeBlanc

"We are indeed much more than what we eat, but what we eat can nevertheless help us to be much more than what we are."
—ADELLE DAVIS, AMERICAN NUTRITIONIST

You may or may not be feeling a little overwhelmed with the basics of how your body works. While learning how the body works and what causes it to malfunction may have been somewhat imposing, I felt this perspective was key to benefiting from the rest of the book.

In these upcoming sections, I'll focus on the foods to incorporate into your diet and why, and the foods you should minimize or avoid. A little education goes a long way, so it should spark several "Aha!" moments. It's a lot easier to justify not eating well when you don't know the power of healthy food. After reading this section, I'm convinced you will change at least one eating habit tomorrow. That alone makes your time investment worthwhile.

We all strive to feel healthy, energetic and alive. But this doesn't happen by accident. It takes deliberate action. None of us can claim to be the exception to this rule. We all need good, wholesome food every day.

Maybe you'll be the one person out of a thousand who eats trash and becomes a centenarian. But the other 99% of us who neglect our nutrition won't be so lucky. Try cleaning up your diet today and maybe making it to one hundred years old won't be a fluke.

So, what does our body need?

1. Whole foods loaded with antioxidants and phytonutrients, such as a variety of organic vegetables and fruits
2. Whole, ancient grains
3. Heart healthy nuts, seeds, beans and legumes
4. Fish, eggs and naturally raised meats
5. Foods void of pesticides

Summed up, anything available during our grandmothers' generation. Agreed that many of our ancestors did not have access to the same variety of food we now have, but what was available was minimally processed and free of synthetic toxins.

Overly-processed foods are to be avoided. They often contain much of what will be vilified later in this section, such as refined sugars and artificial sweeteners. A natural, preferably organic and local diet is key to long lasting, sustainable health.

It's important to remember that the earth provides us with such an abundance of tasty and nutrient-rich foods, that sustaining ourselves on prepackaged products is completely unnecessary. Choose organic produce, legumes, and free-range (organically fed) animal proteins. It's all there for the taking.

If much of what I listed seems like common sense, good. For many, it isn't common sense. Many get health and nutritional information via talk shows, their television, and billboard ads—sponsored by giant corporations who lack sincere interest in the public's health.

Even more villainous are the ads targeted at children. When I see what food marketing has become, it disgusts me. Try watching Saturday morning television with your child, or check out the ads linked to the YouTube videos your kids are watching. I guarantee that you'll be appalled at what we allow companies to push on our children.

While it is important to speak about food, it is also necessary to address one of the most fundamental resources for survival—water. Most of us walking around with symptoms of one ailment or another may very well be chronically dehydrated. Few people realize that chronic dehydration leads to increased cortisol production, which introduces a host of other issues. In many cases, doctors will prescribe drinking more water as the first step in a treatment plan for chronic conditions.

How much water should we be drinking? We've all heard that eight glasses of water per day (approximately 96 ounces) is sufficient. That is a crude estimation. A more accurate recommendation is dependent on knowing one's physical activity, size, and other criteria. For a physically active 200-pound man, 10–12 glasses should hit the spot. For an average-sized woman, aim for 7–8 glasses per day.

The quality of your water is also important to consider. Tap water often contains a plethora of contaminants, including fluoride, chlorine, residual pharmaceutical drugs, and hormones. Water filters and water treatment are necessary to obtain pure, uncontaminated water. There are many options available, but it can be very confusing.

Ikkuma INFO: WHAT WATER IS SAFE?

Carbon vs. Reverse-Osmosis Filtration: There are many options available to filter the water we drink. I'll touch on a couple of the common ones. First, you have carbon filters, which represent your stand-alone pitcher or a faucet mounted device. Carbon filters chemically bond to contaminants in your water. They are effective at reducing contaminants, such as chlorine, lead, mercury and disinfection byproducts; however, they do not adequately deal with inorganic compounds such as fluoride, arsenic and hexavalent chromium. In many municipalities, though controversial, fluoride is added to the drinking water to (ostensibly) improve oral health.

Another more involved filtering solution is reverse osmosis. These systems are typically mounted on the counter or under the sink. Reverse osmosis involves passing water through a fine membrane designed to prevent particles larger than water molecules to pass through. It is effective at filtering out both organic and inorganic compounds. The quality varies greatly from one system to another, and they use much more water than they produce. Reverse osmosis systems use should be limited to cooking and drinking water. There are other products available, such as water softeners, but for your drinking needs, carbon filters and reverse osmosis are your easiest and most affordable options.

Key Foods to Eat

"Living Oceans"—"The vitality of our oceans reflects the level of awareness we are willing to embrace. Let us wake up and work in harmony with the life that seeks to sustain us."

Now that we have a loose framework, I'll deep dive into a several foundational foods to incorporate into your diet, and explain why they are so essential for supporting your vitality. This list is not meant to be exhaustive. It simply highlights the major foods or food groups. Beyond elaborating on these key foods, I will also include some *Ikkuma Top Ten* lists throughout the chapter.

You'll notice that some of these foods are often misunderstood and demonized in the media; the challenge lies in understanding the truth. It's important to scrutinize who is conveying the message and who paid for the report or the research, as many sources of education are sponsored by multinationals with less than genuine motives. There are a lot of players out there who could care less about your health. If you don't manage your health, no one will; least of all, multinational food companies.

i. Eggs

I eat about 14 eggs per week. Admittedly, this may be a little excessive. I'm telling you this because research suggests that eggs are a true superfood. They are high in specific proteins, which, during digestion, get converted by enzymes to peptides, acting as ACE inhibitors—an element common in medications to reduce blood pressure. Eggs have some of the highest levels of biotin in nature. Among several other critical functions, biotin is crucial for cell growth. Eggs are also a good source of lecithin (i.e., a fatty substance used by every cell in our body), which helps lower bad cholesterol. They also contain beta-carotene; effective at maintaining eye and skin health. The deeper yellow, or yellow-orange the yolk, the higher it is in this important vitamin.

Many of the aforementioned vitamins are contained in egg's traditionally-dreaded yolks. Eggs should be organic to ensure quality, and the yolks consumed uncooked (with caution as to their source), as the nutrients in egg yolks are highly perishable and susceptible to heat. Yolks that have been cooked at high temperatures—like when you make scrambled eggs—oxidize. Oxidized cholesterol is directly linked with inflammation, which is believed to be a direct cause of cardiovascular disease[1].

As explained earlier, cholesterol is necessary for every cell in your body and helps produce vitamin D, cell membranes, and hormones. While eggs are relatively high in overall cholesterol, studies have shown that eggs consumed in moderation have little to no effect on bad cholesterol[2].

There are significant differences between commercial eggs and eggs from pastured (i.e., allowed to forage for natural food sources) hens. The potential for salmonella contamination is low when eggs are naturally raised under sanitary conditions. Conversely, due to the disgusting and unsanitary conditions in CAFOs—Caged Animal Feed Operations—the potential for contamination is significantly increased. In 2010 in the U.S., over 500 million eggs were recalled for salmonella contamination that originated from CAFOs[3].

Research also supports that pastured eggs contain less fat and cholesterol than their commercial brethren, and have higher nutrient levels (e.g., omega-3 fatty acids), as per USDA nutrient data[4,5]. We should avoid eggs advertised as being fortified with omega-3s, since they are often derived from hens that are fed from oxidized omega-3 sources.

ii. Meats

I'm not a vegan, nor am I a vegetarian. I find society loves to put people's eating habits in categories. I am of the belief that we have evolved to eat a variety of things on this earth, from meats, fish, and eggs, to broccoli and apples. Up until the great agrarian shift over ten thousand years ago, humans ate what was available. I wrote *Find Your SuperHuman* to help us get back to our roots and take advantage of today's variety and availability of great food.

I do believe, however, that meat overconsumption is one of the key perils to our planet. The greenhouse gasses produced by the meat supply-chain are nothing short of mind-blowing. If we just cut out fast-food burgers from our diets, it would do wonders towards solving climate change.

Though there are many different types of meats one could consume, my condensed list includes red meat, chicken, pork, and lamb. To avoid growth hormones, antibiotics, toxic pesticides and herbicides, it is important to choose free-range (preferably pastured) and organically-fed meats. With an increase in demand for organic and free-range products, these naturally raised meats are now much easier to find.

An important factor to consider when choosing your organic meat is the saturated fat content—a key inflammatory agent when consumed in excess—as red meat is typically high in saturated fat.

Since the topic of meat consumption tends to gravitate toward the pros and cons—in regards to health—of red meat specifically, I will begin there. While I don't believe red meat to be the enemy, it can adversely affect your health if consumed in excess. What is considered excessive? That's where the confusion begins, since, as with most nutritional advice, there is no clear-cut answer. Remember that we are all unique, as I will elaborate on when talking about individualized medicine. Our differences manifest themselves in a variety of ways depending on the foods we eat. There are studies, however, that can help us make a few general conclusions.

A study published in the Archives of Internal Medicine found that life expectancy decreases as meat consumption increases. Many different diseases or 'events' were investigated, such as heart disease, cancer, and stroke. This study was said to be the first to correlate life expectancy to red meat consumption. It tracked over 120,000 people for 28 years; 20% of the participants died during this period. It was estimated that between 7–19% of those who died would have survived during the study if they substituted one daily serving of red meat with fish or chicken. The final recommendation coming out of the study was to eat no more than 2–3 servings of red meat per week[6]. There are many other animal protein sources that can be used as substitutes for red meat, including chicken, eggs, fish, pork, lamb, and marrow.

While studies are imperfect—subjects can misrepresent or forget what they ate, and many other factors not being scrutinized can impact the results—they at least give us a starting point for reflection. Based on what we have heard for years, it seems logical that cutting down on red meat would be prudent. Red meat is harder for the body to digest and, as mentioned, is high in saturated fat and cholesterol. Meat is also void of enzymes, thus depleting the metabolic, food, and digestive enzymes in our body. Enzymes are critical for food digestion, and help to repair and clean up the inside of our body. Red meat is also often charred when cooked, producing carcinogens (i.e., substances capable of causing cancer).

The real issue is cheap and processed red meat. On top of my earlier rant about the environmental perils, many processed types of meat are a nightmare to your health, in that they often contain added nitrites, believed to promote cancer.

Unless you are buying grass-finished cattle, you don't know what's in your meat. In CAFO-raised meat there can be a host of chemicals that aren't fit for humans, such as drug residues, heavy metals, E. coli, various antibiotics, and hormones. Both Europe—since 2006—and the US—since Jan. 1st, 2017—have banned antibiotics for growth promotion in cattle. In 2009, over 29 million pounds of antibiotics were used on livestock in the U.S.[7]

Despite these arguments, singling out red meat as the culprit to our ills is not the solution. As I'll mention throughout the book, focusing on the overconsumption of refined foods and sugar in the Standard American Diet (SAD) is a more worthy pursuit in curing the ails of modern Western society.

iii. Vegetables

Vegetables represent the most nutrient dense foods, with the least calories. They're critical for our survival. Typically, the deeper and darker the color, the higher their antioxidant and phytochemical content. Phytochemicals (or phytonutrients) are loaded with the disease-fighting antioxidants—critical for battling inflammation and illness. One of the most common groups of phytochemicals is called flavonoids.

Vegetables create an internal force field against several chronic diseases. Starchy root vegetables, like sweet potatoes, should make up about 20% of your vegetable intake. Fibrous vegetable consumption, including beloved green leafy vegetables, should make up the remaining 80%. Fibrous vegetables have a lower carbohydrate content and are lower on the glycemic index than starchy root vegetables. Cruciferous vegetables from the brassica family, including cabbage, broccoli, and cauliflower, are some of the most potent cancer-fighting fibrous vegetables available.

You should significantly chew or blend your vegetables. When vegetables are broken down, their enzymes and phytonutrients become more bioavailable, allowing them to be readily absorbed, and in turn, utilized by the body. Smoothies—loaded with fresh vegetables—can be a fantastic way to ensure you're getting plenty of vegetables in your diet.

> *Ikkuma* **INFO: IKKUMA SUPERHUMAN SMOOTHIE**
>
> I have been experimenting with smoothies for decades. This recipe may seem daunting at first, but it isn't that hard if you prepare many of the ingredients ahead of time, in bulk. I'll try to make this as clear as possible. First, I will list what needs to be prepared. I will then give you the recipe.

Preparation:

Fruit & Vegetable Prep: Clean and chop beets, apples, purple cabbage, broccoli, celery, ginger, and kale. You can use whatever vegetables you want, but I stress a good variety (and mostly cruciferous). Chop enough for about one week's worth of smoothies—use trial and error for this one. My experience shows that chopped vegetables, placed in a sealed container with one or two paper towel sheets at the bottom, keep relatively fresh for about one week. This process will save time when making your smoothies.

Seeds of Life **Prep:** Using a coffee grinder, grind sesame, chia, pumpkin, hemp, and flax seeds. Place them in a sealable bag and store in your freezer. Try to keep the mixture relatively fresh by only preparing two to four weeks worth of the mixture.

The Recipe:

Blend the following ingredients in your high-powered blender:

- ¼ cup of organic almond or coconut milk
- 2 cups of fruit and vegetables (see above)
- 1 heaping tablespoon of the *Seeds of Life* mixture
- 20–30 grams of high-quality natural whey protein (or a vegan protein powder, such as sprouted brown rice, pea, or hemp)—approximately 10 grams less for women
- ½ cup of organic frozen berries
- 2 heaping tablespoons of organic yogurt (coconut yogurt can be used if you have a dairy intolerance)
- ¼ tsp cinnamon (helps stabilize blood sugar), ¼ tsp of turmeric powder (flush with cancer-fighting compounds), and 1 tsp of maca root powder for an energy kick (if desired)
- you can also add a serving of your favorite fish oil
- 4-6 ice cubes

One word: AMAZING! This smoothie has incredible body-repairing, immune-system-boosting, gut-populating, cancer-fighting, age-reversing, and antioxidant-flooding goodness.

There is a small caveat: if you don't have a powerful blender, vegetables from the brassica family (e.g., cabbage, broccoli, and kale) may not be fully broken down, and promote gas and cramps. Try to introduce these vegetables slowly. If they remain an issue, substitute them with other fruits or vegetables, such as spinach, and avocado.

Ikkuma's Top 10 Vegetables

Vegetable	Notable Nutrients	Benefits
Spinach	Vitamin K	• bone health. Activates osteocalcin, promoting calcium to bind inside bones • aids in absorbing vitamin D
Onions	Rich in powerful sulfuric compounds and quercetin	• defends against prostate and stomach cancers, and repels osteoclasts, which break down bones • chopping them helps release enzymes
Mushrooms	Selenium, antigen-binding lectins, angiogenesis inhibitors, aromatase inhibitors	• antigen-binding lectins that stick to abnormal cells helping the body identify and attack them • angiogenesis inhibitors inhibit the new blood vessels that tumors need to supply their energy, where aromatase inhibitors help reduce the production of excess estrogen
Kale	Loaded with antioxidants, significant in calcium, iron, vitamins A, C and K, and beta-carotene	• one of the highest concentrations of antioxidants • incredible cancer fighter, loaded with detoxifying enzymes
Sea Vegetables (kelp, wakame, kombu)	Iodine, calcium, iron, and all trace elements in the ocean	• alkalizing (i.e., promote a positive pH), and help to lower cholesterol by binding to cholesterol molecules
Celery	Silica, insoluble fiber	• effective at lowering blood pressure • significant source of fiber
Cabbage	Indoles and anthocyanins	• part of the brassica family • powerful cancer fighter

Broccoli	Isothiocyanates and over a dozen incredible nutrients	• helps neutralize carcinogens • a cancer-fighting all-star
Beets	Bethane, and folate	• supports healthy liver function • inhibits homocysteine, which is a contributor to heart disease • good for athletic endurance
Brussel Sprouts	Folate, potassium, sinigin, and vitamin K	• strong cancer fighter—leverages sinigin to promote apoptosis (i.e., cancer-cell suicide)

iv. Fruit

Fruits are similar to vegetables, in that they contain significant amounts of antioxidants, with the darker colors typically containing the highest concentrations.

The main difference between fruits and vegetables does not lie in their nutritional content, per se, but in their levels of sugar—in the form of fructose. An upcoming section of the book offers an explanation as to why we should scrutinize fructose consumption. Although fructose doesn't spike insulin production, in excess, it can have negative long-term effects. It promotes inflammation, and since only the liver can metabolize fructose, excessive amounts can burden it with added stress.

The reason why fruit in its natural form should not be of concern is due to the fiber contained in the fruits. Fiber acts as a regulator for digesting the fructose in the fruit, representing the main difference between fruit juices and whole fruits. Fruit juices allow the fructose to be absorbed much more quickly than in whole food form. This flood of fructose may not allow your body to properly use up the fructose before it's metabolized, likely storing it as fat[8]. Apart from those who have specific issues like diabetes and metabolic syndrome—who should be moderating their consumption of all sugar sources—I would urge you to eat organic fruits as part of a healthy diet.

It is important to note that since the body quickly digests fruit, it is preferable to fruit either between meals or before a meal. If not, the fruit may sit in your gastrointestinal tract longer than optimal, and potentially start to rot and ferment in the gut. This could manifest itself as indigestion, heartburn, and other mild reactions. Making this a regular habit could cause damage to the microflora in your delicate gut.

Ikkuma's Top 10 Fruits

Fruit	Notable Nutrients	Benefits
Lemon	Minerals, vitamin C	• stimulates the liver and digestion, while acting as an efficient detoxifier
Pineapple	Bromelain, vitamin C, trace elements	• supports digestion and helps fight inflammation • unlike other fruit, can be eaten after a meal
Apples	Various flavonoids (antioxidants)	• helps fight cardiovascular disease and asthma • great for adding sweetness to smoothies
Pears	Similar to apples	• high in fiber and low allergenic potential, for those who do not tolerate apples
Avocados	Heart healthy monounsaturated fats	• very versatile for recipes • can be used as a spread for sandwiches
Blueberries	Anthocyanin (powerful antioxidant)	• known to protect memory • high antioxidant value, i.e., free radical fighter
Cherries	Anthocyanin, quercetin, ellagic acid	• helps support apoptosis (i.e., cancer-cell suicide), and has strong anti-inflammatory properties
Raspberries	Fiber, antioxidants, low caloric	• similar to other berries, with compounds that battle cervical and breast cancer
Strawberries	Similar to other berries	• works to inhibit cancer's progression, and good for memory
Grapefruit	Low glycemic, vitamin C	• shown to reduce insulin resistance • warning: may cause several medications to stay in your system longer

v. Legumes (e.g., Beans)

"Beans, beans the magical fruit, the more we eat, the more we toot!" We all remember this rhyme growing up as kids. Yes, beans tend to give us a little gas, but beans and other legumes should be part of a healthy diet. Legumes contain a mixture of protein, carbohydrates, and loads of fiber. The high fiber content of these foods is key for normalizing cholesterol, stabilizing blood sugars, and promoting healthy bowel function. We should be having as many bowel movements as we do major meals. If you do 'number 2' less than twice per day, maybe you need more beans.

The protein, or amino acid content, in beans is not as complete as that found in animal protein, so we consider it an incomplete protein. When combined with a whole grain, such as brown rice, millet or quinoa (technically a seed)—which also contain an incomplete but complementary profile of amino acids—they form a relatively complete protein. These pairings are important for vegetarians and vegans, as complete proteins are vital for hormone and neurotransmitter synthesis, muscle repair, immunity, and several other crucial processes.

Back to the gas, which is (at least to some extent) preventable. The oligosaccharides (i.e., a sugar in the covering of the bean) found in beans is the main cause of the gas we may experience after eating beans. Since our bodies only absorb about 50% of the bean's carb calories we consume, there is a lot of fuel left over to produce gas. Inherently difficult to digest, oligosaccharides ferment in the lower intestine—acting as prebiotics—and cause gas. Prebiotics are indigestible foods that feed the beneficial bacteria in the gastrointestinal tract. More beneficial bacteria equals a healthier gut, and a healthier you.

Soaking dried beans in water overnight can reduce the gas-causing effects of beans. In the morning, discard the water, rinse, and cook the beans in fresh water. Another way to decrease this displeasing side effect is to start with small amounts of more easily digestible beans, such as lentils, mung, adzuki and black beans. The larger beans, such as chickpeas, and kidney beans, typically produce more gas.

Moving on to other common legumes, I have to begin with a peanut warning—yes, peanuts are legumes. Peanuts can be contaminated with a mold, called aflatoxin, which is carcinogenic. They should not be eaten raw. We are also aware of the growing intolerance to peanuts, so be careful when dealing with these legumes.

Legumes contain an abundance of available nutrition, such as cancer-fighting phytonutrients and polyphenols. As stated in an *American Journal of Epidemiology* study[9], which took place over a period of twenty years, people who ate more than two servings of legumes weekly, versus less than one serving, were 47% less likely to develop colon cancer[10].

vi. Whole Grains

Dr. Angelina and I argued about grains for the longest time. In the end, I conceded and now support the advice that the right grains can be part of a balanced diet. In fact, the carbohydrates within grains are the primary fuel for the human body. However, I can't stress enough that not all grains are created equal. It's most often the simple carbohydrates contained in refined grains—the villains of this story—that are shortchanging your health.

Complex or unrefined grains are preferred, as they contain both the starch (carbohydrates), fiber, and germ component of the grain. These components provide our bodies with a more sustainable energy source, along with a lower glycemic load (i.e., a lesser effect on increasing blood glucose levels) than refined grains. The whole grain is also more nutrient-rich than its refined offspring, containing B vitamins, vitamin E, and many minerals such as magnesium, zinc, iron, as well as calcium and selenium (in select grains).

Fiber consumption is typically low in the Standard American Diet, which is likely a major contributor to many chronic Western conditions like high cholesterol, gallstones, constipation, and colon cancer, to name a few.

For these reasons, I (cautiously) support incorporating whole grains into your diet. I say cautiously because one must be on the lookout for gluten-containing grains, as their consumption may lead to gut inflammation. This is an important precaution to take, as the rates of gluten intolerance are on the rise. Focus on whole, gluten-free grains, such as brown rice, millet, oats, quinoa, amaranth, and buckwheat. Common gluten-containing whole grains include whole wheat, barley, spelt and rye.

vii. Fish

Little disgusts me more than how we've polluted our waters. Two-thirds of the surface of our precious earth is water. We have somehow—in the past two centuries—dumped so many toxins into the oceans that we've chemically altered the billions of fish upon which we rely. It's appalling and entitled of us to believe we have the right to squander such a critical natural resource. The fish we eat will never be the same.

Despite how badly we have messed up our oceans, numerous studies have shown that eating 2–3 servings of fish per week is still beneficial. Along with having low concentrations of saturated fats, the benefits of eating fish stem from their high level of healthy fats (i.e., omega-3s), protein, and vitamins. Fish can also be excellent sources of iodine, iron, and choline. Put all these anti-inflammatory nutritional powerhouses together, and you're left with food that lowers the risk of cardiovascular disease, cancer, stroke, diabetes, and Alzheimer's.

Sardines and wild Alaskan salmon are particularly high in omega-3s with relatively low levels of mercury. Take note that farmed salmon is inferior to wild salmon. Farmed salmon can be fed grain, resulting in significantly less heart-healthy omega-3s, and more omega-6s. Moreover, the 'net pens' where they are farmed are similar to CAFOs, but in water. Largely due to the unsanitary conditions in these net pens, farmed salmon are regularly fed antibiotics to ward off disease. The Environmental Working Group—a leading environmental health research and advocacy organization—found that "an average farmed salmon had 16 times the dioxin-like PCBs found in wild salmon."[11] In restaurants, farmed fish is my biggest concern. Always ask the server if the fish is wild or farmed.

As I alluded to earlier, a relevant issue with fish consumption is their concentration of heavy metals, including mercury. Larger and longer living predatory fish will typically have the highest concentration of heavy metals and toxins. These fish eat smaller fish, resulting in a compounding effect, with toxins accumulating in their fatty tissue. Tuna steaks and swordfish are perfect examples. Canned white and flaked tuna should also be avoided. Skipjack tuna, which is smaller and much lower in mercury, is preferable. Wild salmon is also relatively low in mercury, especially wild Alaskan salmon. Regardless of how the fish is prepared, the mercury content will not be affected.

It is also good to note, that although all fish have mercury, they are also high in selenium, which is a potent chelator of mercury (i.e. binds to and helps rid it from your body). You want to stick to fish low in mercury to allow for the selenium to mitigate mercury's detrimental effects.

While choosing which fish to eat is not an exact science, it is important to be aware of which types to avoid. See the table below for a list of some popular fish with relatively high mercury content (Source: FDA):

(High) Mercury Content in Various Fish

Fish	Mean Mercury Concentration (ppm)
Grouper	0.448
Sablefish (or Black Cod)	0.361
Chilean Sea Bass	0.354
Tuna (canned albacore)	0.350
Halibut	0.241
Snapper	0.166
Perch (freshwater)	0.150
Tuna (skipjack)	0.144

Since mercury accumulates in fatty tissue there is not necessarily a safe limit, so try to limit the exposure as much as possible. The following table lists some popular fish with relatively low mercury content (Source: FDA):

(Low) Mercury Content in Various Fish

Scallops	0.003
Salmon (canned)	0.008
Clams	0.009
Shrimp	0.009
Oysters	0.012
Sardine	0.013
Tilapia	0.013
Anchovies	0.017
Salmon	0.022

viii. Nuts and Seeds

Raw nuts and seeds are nutritional powerhouses, packed full of minerals such as magnesium, zinc, potassium, and calcium. Often high in protein, they are also a good source of healthy fat, and fat-soluble vitamins A, E, D, and K. They are, however, high in fat calories, with each gram of fat containing nine calories—that's over twice the amount you'll find in proteins and carbohydrates. Due to their high fat content, some people may find nuts and seeds difficult to digest.

> *Ikkuma* **INFO: TOP DIGESTION TIPS**
>
> 1. Eat while you are relaxed and take your time. Being in a relaxed state will optimize digestion. Digestion begins in the mouth, so chew your food well.
> 2. Avoid drinking water or any liquids while you are eating. Liquids will dilute your digestive juices, leading to gastric reflux, gas, and bloating. Also avoid large amounts of liquids within a half an hour before and after eating. If you need liquid to wash down your food, refer to Tip #1!
> 3. Eat simple meals and avoid eating large amounts of food in one sitting. Simple food combinations promote healthy and efficient digestion. A large amount of food at once slows digestion, which can lead to indigestion and fatigue.
> 4. Eat fruit on its own and between meals. Fruit digests very quickly and can ferment if eaten after a large meal, leading to gas and bloating.
> 5. Soak beans and legumes to improve their breakdown. Introduce beans and legumes into your diet slowly, and in small amounts.

Although nuts are excellent sources of nutrients, they are also high in omega-6 fats. Though these fats are necessary for optimal metabolic functioning of the body, when the ratio of omega-6s to omega-3s is thrown off kilter, trouble can arise. Again, eat nuts in moderation, and consume ample sources of omega-3s to keep your body in balance.

To Be, or Not To Be... Organic

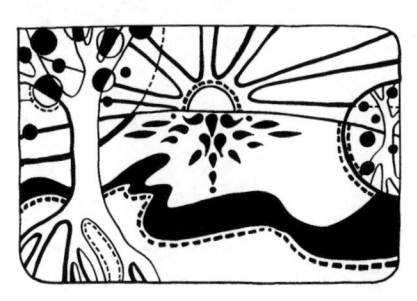

"One World"—Health and vibrancy echoes out in a world that knows its wholeness. We are forever connected to every one and every thing. There is only One World, it is our duty to nurture it.

Let's talk about organic food. Organic has become a hot topic these days. I've heard—ad nauseam—the arguments against organic food. None have yet to sway my opinion. I can't have a rational argument with people who think that chemically doused food is equivalent to naturally cultivated food. "Oh, but studies show that conventionally grown food is nutritionally equivalent." I'm sorry, but I'm calling bullshit on that one. Read on and you tell me.

Don't even get me started on Genetically Modified foods (GMOs). If chemical companies had nothing to hide, then their legal bills wouldn't be greater than the GDP of some small countries. It's time for us to wake up and ask more questions. I'll soon address GMOs in greater detail.

One of the major growth sectors in the food industry is organics. Certified organic foods are produced without the use of synthetic chemical fertilizers and pesticides, are not irradiated, have no chemical food additives, nor do they contain any genetically modified components.

There are many certified-organic regulating bodies with varying regulatory requirements, some of which are stricter than others. One common and trusted organic certification is *USDA Organic*.

The majority of people still view organics as a luxury for the wealthy or an ideology supported by hippies. It's hard to blame the general public for this distorted view of organics, in that huge chemical companies have inundated the public with propaganda, touting the benefits and safety of conventional farming, and the ineffectiveness of organic food.

Please note that we are often sold on the term 'natural' as being synonymous with organic. In no way does the term natural imply the same benefits as organic food. The natural claim is highly unregulated, allowing companies to take liberties using the term. Foods that are termed natural can be genetically modified, use synthetic pesticides, and may contain food additives. In order to get the true benefits of natural, you need to buy foods labeled as Certified Organic or better yet, learn the practices of a local farm that follows organic practices.

Before we get into the heart of the organics versus genetically modified organisms conversation, let's paint a picture of our existing chemically dependent food supply. The estimated current use of pesticides in the U.S. has surpassed 1 billion pounds per year, or approximately 4 pounds of pesticides per person[12]. Alarmingly, these pesticides are finding their way into our bodies, in that, practically everyone has some trace of pesticides in their blood. Pesticides are even found in amniotic fluid, meaning that our babies are being born with these chemicals present[13].

At the heart of this chemical dependency are genetically modified seeds, used for the majority of conventionally grown foods. These seeds are on the Generally Regarded As Safe (GRAS) list, and considered equivalent to non-GMO. This equivalency affords the companies selling these patented seeds the ability to distribute them freely without the necessity of proving long-term safety. As such, there have been no long-term studies done on how they affect our health. Chemical companies spend billions of dollars to ensure the government maintains this status quo. They actively lobby against labeling of GMO foods, and dismiss the need for long-term studies. A public more informed of the detriments of GMO terrifies chemical companies because they know that once people become aware of the severe toll their products may take on our health and that of the environment, they may avoid consuming them.

To start decoding the organic versus GMO mystery, we'll first get into the weeds (excuse the pun) on GMOs, and then end on a strong note with organics. Sifting through the rhetoric is tricky at best. The focus will be on what we know now, and why we should be wary of what we don't know.

GMOs and Chemical Farming

In the next several pages I'm going to paint a picture using existing studies of why you should be concerned that GMO foods have become so ubiquitous in today's society.

I don't buy into conspiracy theories. I'm a pragmatic engineer and businessman by trade, who has worked for multinational food and beverage companies. I've seen this issue from both sides, and one side is not pretty. We're flipping a coin for our future. We're, for the first time, messing with evolution and the delicate interdependencies of all living things.

Just look at the companies controlling this space. Look and ask yourself if they care about the future of society. I'm sure many of their employees do, but what drives these companies has little to do with the state of the world twenty years from now. Make your conclusions. I'm personally frightened at what comes next if we don't make it difficult for these companies to stay in business.

Scope of the Epidemic

GMO is an abbreviation for Genetically Modified Organism. They are organisms that have undergone specific gene manipulation, meaning that specific genes are spliced with certain chemicals or toxins to achieve a desired trait. One common reason for this is to protect certain crops from specific herbicides and pesticides, such as glyphosates (e.g., Round Up).

This agricultural transformation started getting traction back in 1980, when the U.S. Supreme Court, in a close decision, allowed companies to genetically engineer seeds. This decision forced farmers to buy their chemical resistant seeds from massive food and chemical companies. 'Roundup Ready' seeds, which survive exposure to abhorrent amounts of pesticides, are the most commonly used GM seeds.

Following this critical 1980 decision, farming and agriculture would never be the same. What was a fairly natural and family run business was now in the hands of a few powerful chemical companies.

Three major crops grown with GM seeds are corn, soy, and canola. It is estimated that over 75% of all processed foods contain GMOs of some sort. In the U.S., it is estimated that approximately 90% of all conventional crops are grown using GM seeds. In addition to the ballooning rates of GM seed use, is the concern of GM crops cross-contaminating (i.e., infiltrating) non-GM crops—pollen travels in the wind, so being in proximity to a GM crop, poses a contamination risk. Cross-contamination is an issue because once GM seeds invade a non-GM crop, it is tough to eliminate this new strain from the fields.

Many farmers don't want to grow GM plants, yet once a crop has been contaminated with the GM seed, not only it is difficult to eradicate the GM seed, but they are now beholden to the chemical companies and can be fined if they do not pay for the seed. Without even choosing to use GM seeds, farmers can end up paying giant chemical companies for seeds they didn't want in the first place. This demented situation is beyond reproach. Utter bullshit! Shame on the lobbyists who've convinced the government to allow this to happen.

The approval of GM alfalfa is of particular concern because insects pollinate alfalfa, opening the door for cross-contamination of GM and non-GM crops hundreds of miles apart.

Several European countries—France and Hungary, to name a couple—have gone as far as fully or partially banning the use of genetically modified seeds. It is encouraging that dozens of countries—who are employing a much more precautionary approach—do not support the U.S. principle of 'safe until proven unsafe.'

Companies around the world are also starting to treat GM foods differently from country to country. In the European Union, two of the most high-profile companies in the world, Walmart and McDonalds, boast all locations or subsidiaries as GMO-free. They ostensibly do this because, since 1997, the European Union requires labeling of GMO foods, as is stated on the European Commission Health and Consumers website:

"The EU recognizes the consumers' right to information and labeling as a tool for making an informed choice. Since 1997 Community legislation has made labeling of GM food mandatory for:

- products that consist of GMO or contain GMO;
- products derived from GMO but no longer containing GMO if there is still DNA or protein resulting from the genetic modification present".

Am I the only one who finds this blatantly hypocritical? These companies brag about being GMO-free, yet in the U.S. where they don't need to label, they freely serve GMO foods. Once again, it's all about making cheap food at all costs. Do you think they would have stopped serving GMO food in Europe if the labeling requirements hadn't changed?

There are over sixty countries worldwide that require GMO labeling. Amazingly, the U.S. and Canada still do not require any labeling of GMO foods. In the U.S., California drafted Proposition 37, which would have forced companies to label GMO foods—not surprisingly, it wasn't approved. The proposition was propelled by the belief that if people knew what was in these genetically modified foods, they would most likely choose to avoid them. Companies would then, to stay in business, opt to replace these ingredients with healthier, proven alternatives. The powerful chemical company lobby spent millions to defeat the proposition. The purported increase in food costs became their central defense. Once again, it came down to money.

The Health Dangers of GMOs and the Chemicals Involved

While it has been very difficult for scientists to develop a 'cause and effect' argument for the impacts of GMO on humans, there are a couple of interesting trends that are important to be aware of: asthma increased by 75% from 1980–1994[14], and food allergies have gone up nearly 20% in a recent decade[15].

While there may well be other explanations, we can't dismiss the obvious correlations between the chemical changes in our food chain and the increasing incidences of adverse health conditions. The sad reality is that we don't specifically know what's affecting our health and the health of our children. The reason we have no clue what is truly causing these trends in children is because they're exposed to so many chemicals. Too many variables exist, making it nearly impossible to narrow-down the culprits. One thing we do know is that without sweeping change, the generations that follow are in for a rough ride.

To give you a sense of what is lurking in your GMOs, let's look at Bt corn, which represents over two-thirds of all corn grown in the U.S. Bt corn is the corn used in the U.S. that is resistant to the herbicide

Roundup. The protective ingredient inserted into Bt corn seeds is Bt toxin. Companies inject this in the seeds to destroy the rootworms and other insects when they consume the corn. After ingesting Bt toxin, insects' stomachs effectively explode.

It was initially believed that Bt toxin could not survive in the human stomach. However, it is now being found in human blood. In a study at the University of Sherbrooke in Quebec, Bt toxin was found in the blood of 93% of pregnant women tested, 80% of the umbilical cord blood, and 67% of non-pregnant women. Apparently, our digestive tract is not entirely eliminating this toxin. No one can definitively understand what havoc this is wreaking on our gut flora, and immune systems.

Although health issues related to GMOs are relatively unsubstantiated, there is growing research showing their potential links to cancer. One monumental French study found serious links between 'Roundup Ready' crops and large cancerous tumors—along with damage to several organs—in rats. Although this was not a human study, it highlights the potential dangers of the consumption of GM foods in mammals[16].

Beyond the potential dangers of the GMO crops themselves, there are studies showing the impact of common herbicides (used on GMO crops) on the human body. A study performed at the University of Caen has found that glyphosates are toxic to human cells[17]. Another study by two Swedish scientists has found a clear link between glyphosates and non-Hodgkin's lymphoma[18]. Another study has shown that glyphosates also decrease liver enzymes in the body, which then affects the body's ability to detoxify—a vicious circle[19]. Presumably, this is just the tip of the iceberg. Science is shedding more and more light on glyphosates and the potential dangers they pose to humans.

Fearing that consumers become more aware of what's in their food, and the related health risks, has prompted intense lobbying by major U.S. chemical and biotech firms against the labeling of GM foods. They have been successful thus far, in that there is still no mandatory labeling of GM foods in the U.S. To defeat Proposition 37, in California, it is estimated that the GMO lobby spent tens of millions of dollars to sway the public vote. It worked. Over 50% of Californians sided with the chemical companies. I'm curious who voted against GMO labeling? That alone is alarming. That alone should open your eyes to how powerful and influential these companies have become.

There are several arguments that companies use to support the use of GMO foods. Let's look at a few and analyze the claims:

- *'Genetically modified organisms are equivalent to non-GMOs'*: this argument relies on the fact that seeds have been cross-bred for thousands of years, seemingly without any detrimental effects to humans. GMOs are different than crossbred organisms. In GMOs, toxins, animal genes, and bacteria, are being spliced into these new GM seeds. We have yet to witness the long-term effects of this novel approach to seed 'design'.
- *'Genetically modified organisms produce better yields'*: this is unfounded. In fact, it has been demonstrated that organically-raised food is more resistant to adverse growing conditions, of which we have experienced plenty in the past several growing years. The practice of organic growing may be more labor intensive, but several studies have shown that organic farming out-produces genetically engineered crops[20].
- *'Genetically modified foods are as nutritious as organically raised crops'*: Although GM seeds may survive extensive pesticide exposure, it does not imply that the plant will be robust and healthy. Fertilizers typically contain forms of phosphates, nitrates, and potassium, amongst other inorganic components. If the soil is absent of organic nutrition, and the seeds grow because they simply have the three necessary components required for growth, will they be very nutritious? Will they contain all the nutrients our bodies need to thrive? If you feed your child candy and milk for years, they may grow, but they won't be healthy.

In the end, it's up to you to decide how you want to sustain your body. What we do know, regardless of nutritional content, is that GMOs have a higher pesticide content. For example, Roundup contains surfactants that allow it to stick to, and penetrate, the plant it is protecting. Therefore, when we consume these plants, we are allowing these embedded chemicals into our bodies, where they have the potential to cross our blood-brain barriers. As the use of these chemicals increases, so too does their concentration in our bodies.

While the train seems to have left the station, I am still wary of the presence of GMOs in our food supply. The long-term effects of GMOs on human health and the environment are still largely unknown. Scientists admit that it is nearly impossible to understand the long-term consequences of an organism when you are splicing it with viruses, bacteria, toxins, and various allergenic substances. So, we may be creating entirely new toxins and allergens, with potentially negative impacts to our health. Is this a risk upon which you are willing to bet your health? The time for half-measures has passed. We need to do what we can to revamp our food chain, and aggressively investigate the potential impacts of Genetically Modified Organisms.

Ikkuma INFO: SOME OF THE WORST GMOS

- *Corn:* it's estimated that over 85% of the corn produced in the U.S. is Genetically Modified, with 'Roundup Ready' seeds being responsible for most of the crop. Corn is also one of the more ubiquitous foods in the grocery store, finding itself in most processed foods in the form of high fructose corn syrup. Solid arguments have been made, supporting that HFCS is one of the leading causes of obesity
- *Soy:* nearly all of the soy produced in the U.S. is genetically modified. Approximately 100 million pounds of glyphosates are used on soybeans
- *Sugar:* in the U.S., since 2009, there have been sugar beets designed to resist herbicides
- *Aspartame:* along with its potential for increasing the risk of specific neurological issues, such as seizures and anxiety, aspartame is often produced using genetically modified bacteria
- *Papayas:* genetically modified papayas have been growing in Hawaii since 1999. Although the European Union does not allow their entry to the market, they are sold in North America
- *Canola:* over 90% of canola oil comes from genetically modified rapeseed. Canola can be found in several packaged foods
- *Cotton:* cotton oil originating from cotton grown in India and China is

> particularly harmful
> - *Dairy:* rBGH (recombinant bovine growth hormone) is found in a significant percentage of U.S. dairy cows but banned in over 25 countries. Steer clear
> - *Zucchini and Yellow Squash:* these vegetables join the ranks of those modified to resist viruses

And What About the Environment?

"Soil Dynamics"—The complex life and vitality beneath our feet is the foundation for the life and vitality we seek in our lives. Living soil equals a vital world.

By now you know that in the U.S., the majority of all conventional crops are born of GM seeds and that these crops are often doused with the pesticide Roundup. As a result, pests are becoming increasingly resistant to these pesticides, forcing farmers to use more chemicals to get the job done.

A 16-year study published in Environmental Sciences Europe found that, although there was a slight dip in herbicide use between 1996-1999 (approx. 2%), the usage of herbicides has spiked due to the emergence of superweeds. These weeds have forced farmers to continually scale up their use of herbicides to maintain yields, as pests have developed a resistance to glyphosates (the active chemical ingredient in the herbicide Roundup). The Environmental Protection Agency (EPA) has also stated that the rootworms may be slowly developing resistance to Roundup Ready produce[21].

As can be seen in much of nature, organisms may succumb to

chemicals in the short term, but evolution catches up, and we need to continue scaling up the response. Eventually, these pests will be so resilient that even if we were to revert to traditional methods of control, dealing with them may prove too difficult.

Fuelled by the increasing quantities of chemicals needed to grow our food, poisons find their way into the soil and can build up over time. The runoff from the soil then enters our waters, which is either used as drinking water, used to water crops—approximately 60% of all fresh water used in the U.S. is used for agriculture[22]—or paves a path of destruction in the environment, particularly by compromising aquatic life. The EPA reported that "more than half of all (U.S.) rivers are unable to sustain life"! Let that one digest for a few minutes. And reports of the chemicals making their way into our drinking water are not anecdotal. Alarmingly, traces of these chemicals are indeed being found in urine samples[23].

Chemical farming's impact on the environment doesn't stop at poisoning our soil and water; it can be found everywhere, especially in animals. For instance, due to the extensive use of antibiotics in raising our cattle, we are finding newly antibiotic-resistant bacteria in our food. Moreover, the *American Academy of Environmental Medicine* has published various animal studies showing infertility, accelerated aging, insulin regulation issues, and organ changes[24].

These are not merely observations; they are fact. There are several other animal studies showing causation between the consumption of GMO foods, and disease in animals. Among them:

- Finamore A, Roselli M, Britti S, et al., *"Intestinal and peripheral immune response to MON 810 maize ingestion in weaning and old mice."* J Agric. Food Chem. 2008, 56(23):11533–11539
- Malatesta M, Boraldi F, Annovi G, et al. *"A long-term study on female mice fed on a genetically modified soybean: effects on liver aging."* Histochem Cell Biol. 2008, 130:96–977
- Velimirov A, Binter C, Zentek J. *"Biological effects of transgenic maize NK603xMON810 fed in long term reproduction studies in mice.",* Report-Federal Ministry of Health, Family, and Youth. 2008

Often when we speak of environmental effects, we're referring to impacts on water, soil and animals. We rarely look beyond this, yet one of the most disturbing trends that we are witnessing is the decimation of our honeybee population. This trend is cause for incredible concern, as Albert Einstein realized when he stated, "If the bee disappeared off the face of the earth, man would only have four years left to live."

As discussed in the documentary, *Vanishing of the Bees* directed by Langworthy and Henein, honeybees are crucial for the sustainability of our food supply. They are pollinating workhorses responsible for over 30% of our food supply and pollinate over 100 crops and flowers in the U.S. alone. Other critical byproducts from honeybees' efforts are wax and honey, used for several applications including cosmetics and medicine.

Due to Colony Collapse Disorder (CCD), they are disappearing at an alarming rate. One of the leading causes of this phenomenon is believed to be the massive surge of GMOs. It is believed that a new class of insecticides called neonicotinoids is compromising the immune systems of honeybees. These pesticides get into the soil and groundwater and accumulate, making their way into the plant, including the nectar. Bees ingesting this pesticide have their central nervous systems irreversibly compromised, causing them to die at an alarming rate.

Unfortunately, since it is effective at eradicating insects, virtually all of the genetically engineered Bt corn grown is sprayed with this type of pesticide. Is it a coincidence that honeybee populations starting dwindling after these new pesticides were approved? The European Commission has imposed an indefinite ban on various neonicotinoids, citing growing concerns over their effect on the bee population[25]. Even the EPA admits that pesticides are probably the cause of the dwindling bee population, which we depend on for our food. This provides another compelling reason to avoid GMOs and support organic farming. I've read my book at least two hundred times and still can't get over some of these facts. I can't believe that we allow these practices to continue.

Organic Farming

I think I've made it pretty clear what I think of GMO foods. By this point, you should have a fairly clear picture of what we're dealing with in regards to GMOs and chemical farming. Let's now move onto the state of organic today.

Organic farmland represents less than 1% of the total farmland in the U.S. In Europe, this number is approximately 4%[26]. It's disappointing and terrifying to see how little of our land is protected from harmful chemicals. We are far from embracing the sustainable nature of growing organically. In organic farming, everything is in symbiosis. Animals eat the plants and fertilize the ground, allowing new plants to flourish. Everything has evolved to work together, without synthetic chemicals.

> *Ikkuma* **SPOTLIGHT: EARTHBOUND FARMS**
>
> Earthbound Farms was founded by Myra Goodman and her husband. With a group consisting of over 150 certified organic farmers, they sell fruits and vegetables grown on over 33,000 acres of farmland. Without any government subsidies (unlike many conventional farmers who rely on the *Farm Bill*), they run a profitable business, keeping over 10 million pounds of chemical fertilizers and over 300 thousand pounds of chemical pesticides from contaminating the environment. Lastly, the carbon stored in the healthy, vibrant soil is equivalent to removing 7500 cars from the roads. Can organic farming be viable when it becomes a large-scale operation? Earth Farms illustrates that it can.

Let's cut through the negative propaganda from chemical companies regarding organics and look at some results of a *Farm Systems Trial* run by the Rodale Institute (an American non-profit organization that supports studies in organic farming):

- in times of average precipitation, organic farming yields are comparable to synthetic methods. However, in times of drought and floods, the deep root structure of organic crops produces better yields
- organic corn and soy crops use approximately 30% less fossil fuels than their GMO counterparts
- economic return is relatively the same for both methods of farming
- due to microbials in the soil, there is significant carbon sequestration associated with organic farming. Simply put, while

the earth has been designed to store carbon dioxide, the use of chemicals renders it useless

Ikkuma INFO: CLIMATE CHANGE

Organically grown crops have very deep and healthy root structures. Mycorrhizal fungi grow on these roots. When present, these fungi sequester carbon in the soil. Unfortunately along with the pesticides, fungicides are often used, which destroy these fungi. It is estimated that if all crops were converted to organic crops, through the great work of these fungi, we would see an instant and significant reduction in atmospheric carbon.

Organic... The Right Choice

Let's summarize why organic is the choice we should all make:

- conventional farming is artificially cheaper, in that it's subsidized
- synthetic chemicals are toxic and not necessary
- chemicals poison the soil, food, water, and our bodies
- chemicals destroy beneficial microbials in our soils
- there is no proven safe limit for toxins
- organic food is healthier and safer—no antibiotics, no GMOs, and no synthetic chemicals
- organic often tastes better
- organic can feed the world in a sustainable way—long term

Let's not kid ourselves—chemical farming isn't about feeding the world, it's about increasing profits. Altruism doesn't increase a chemical company's stock price; uncontrolled chemical farming does. They would have you believe that genetically modified seeds are the saviors of the present food shortages in underdeveloped countries. This is not the case. Tragically, with the advent of GMOs and conventional meat production methods, such as Caged Animal Farm Operations (CAFOs), we have gone down a road that threatens our health, the health of our children, and the survival of our planet.

Chemical industries are not only ignoring the full impact of their products, they may be actively hiding the truth from the public. Millions of dollars each year are spent lobbying for decreased governmental scrutiny, and on funding isolated studies used to convince the public that their chemicals, and GMOs, are safe for consumption. The fact is, if GMOs were safe, these companies wouldn't have to spend so much time and money fighting against GMO labeling. Along with the millions of dollars spent defeating Proposal 37 in California, another recent example of the industry's paranoia involves a lawsuit threatened by a chemical company versus the state of Virginia for a similar proposal.

As Maria Rodale argues in *Organic Manifesto*[27], the U.S's controversial *Farm Bill*—a federal government food and agricultural policy that is passed every five years by the U.S. Congress—creates an even more unfair fight between the defenseless organic movement and huge multinational chemical companies. This $275 billion Farm Bill almost entirely subsidizes the conventional chemical-based method of farming, encouraging the proliferation of GMOs. If not for this massive subsidy, and if the total cost of chemical farming were understood (i.e., the cleanup of contaminated water, land, and soil, and the cost to the health care system) then organic farming would be a more widely accepted long-term option.

The organic movement is all about the long game. What goes in the soil gets in the crops, which is eaten by animals, and us, while we then eat the animals as well. Organic farming helps maintain the quality of the soil, which means we're getting all of the nutrients from our food that our bodies require. GMO farming typically depletes the soil of nutrition, making plants and animals, and in turn making us, nutrient deficient. Though you may not be able to physically see minerals, nutrients, and phytonutrients, it is important to remember that they are vital for our health and wellbeing. You may not immediately notice the difference between organic and conventional broccoli, but over time your body may. You may dispute the adverse impacts that chemical farming has on the environment but future generations will not have that luxury.

If you could see the chemicals in, and on your food, wouldn't you feel differently? We know the right thing to do, yet we convince ourselves that our choices do not have an impact on our health or the health of our planet.

Despite the overwhelming evidence that GMO food is potentially dangerous to our existence, they are still not adequately tested. Another report released in June 2012 by Dr. Michael Antoniou of King's College London School of Medicine in the UK, highlighted that "Research studies show that genetically modified crops have harmful effects on animals in feeding trials…"

Since when have we treated our food in terms of 'innocent until proven guilty'? It's time to insist on a change. Don't just talk about it. Make changes today. Sadly, due to its ubiquity in our food chain, even if we finally unlock the secrets behind GMO's long-term impacts, it would take a monumental effort to reverse the damage.

It is essentially impossible that organics are not better for our health and the health of the environment. The only question left is what is your health worth? With just over 5% of an American household's expenditures allocated to food, it's hard to believe that cost is the issue. We spend money on the latest smartphones, eat at expensive restaurants, and enjoy countless other creature comforts, but we convince ourselves that organic food is not worth the extra expense. So, maybe it's an opportunity cost argument, in that, if you buy organic food you can't afford the latest electronic gadget.

For the fun of it, let's play this out. In the U.S., the average in-home spend on food hovers at around 5.5%. Let's estimate that the average household salary before taxes is approximately $50k. Do some quick math, and you'll see that the total cost of food for in-home consumption hovers around $2750. Even if the cost of organic food was 50% more than conventional food (most report it costing approximately 20% more), you're only talking about an extra $1375 per year. Are you willing to play Russian roulette with the health of your whole family for under $1500 per year? That's the question. Ignore the rest of the rhetoric. Just answer that one question.

Eating wholesome, natural, organic foods is the safest choice until we know unequivocally that GMO foods are safe for humans and the environment. Support your local organic farmers. Stop supporting GMOs and massive chemical companies. Demand organic!

So What About Supplements?

I've talked at length about the good, wholesome foods we should be putting in our bodies for a reason... so you eat them. Don't take this section on supplements as a carte-blanche to start disregarding wholesome nutrition from your food, while thinking supplements will fulfill your nutritional needs. They won't. They can, however, serve a few purposes. I'll give you the basics on how to potentially incorporate supplements into your diet.

I define supplements as substances you consume to provide you with the nutrients of which you may be deficient, or to give you support in a particular area of need. Due to the current state of farming, agriculture, and food production, even if we were all doing our best to eat a proper diet, some of us would still require supplementation.

According to a study in The Journal of the American Medical Association from 2002, the poor quality of soil is making it increasingly difficult to obtain all your nutrients from diet alone, a reality exacerbated by the fact that significantly less than 5% of our food supply is organic. Moreover, the majority of the public is not eating properly. As per the U.S. government's survey *Healthy People 2010*, only 3% of Americans eat a meager three servings of vegetables daily. Hence, it seems difficult for this population to meet their nutritional needs without some supplementation. Vitamin D is a good example of a nutrient of which you may have a deficiency, unless you get a lot of sunlight.

Although supplements provide an apparent way out of our nutritional inadequacies, they are not a panacea. Before discussing the whole-food supplements that could add benefits to your diet, I would like to discuss the little-known topic of 'Nutritionism'.

Nutritionism

> *"In wilderness I sense the miracle of life, and behind it our scientific accomplishments fade to trivia."*
> —CHARLES LINDBERGH, AMERICAN AVIATOR

I turned 45 this year. I was born in the 1970s, during the golden years of the processed food revolution (though, in my opinion, devolution seems to be a more accurate term). The way we received our nutrition would forever be altered, making the food from our grandparents' era almost alien. The advent of these manufactured food products blatantly disregarded the health of the public for the sake of corporate profits. Population growth was not sufficient enough to satisfy corporations' desire for profit, so they either had to convince us to eat more or make food a lot cheaper. In the end, both occurred, creating a painful irony; while health claims were used to boost sales, companies sacrificed the quality of these products in the interest of lowering their cost. I know this first hand from my years working for a multinational food company.

Unfortunately, in allowing ourselves to be romanced by attractive packaging, health claims, and convenience, we had naïvely given scientists and corporations permission to dictate what was good and bad for us—and we continue to do that to this day. Truthfully, have we made it easy or hard for this to happen? What level of scepticism have you exercised when faced with grandiose health claims? Why do we continue to take things at face value? Have we not yet had the impetus to be even a little bit curious about what goes into our food?

Reductionism was one of the key theories that gave this shift towards fortified foods, the nominal credibility it needed. Simply explained, the term reductionism refers to the devaluing of the contextual aspect of an object, relying solely on the characteristics of its parts. As stated by Michael Pollan in his book *In Defense of Food*[28], nutritionism is a form of reductionism in that it defines foods as "the sum of their nutrient parts."

In other words, it posits that the nutritional value of food can be measured solely by its individual components (i.e., vitamins, minerals, and so on), rather than how those components work together synergistically within the whole food. Food scientists use this application of reductionism so that they may mechanically recreate specific, appealing components within their manufactured products. Unfortunately, a human-made version of a mineral or vitamin, standing alone, out of context from its original whole food source may never be nutritionally sufficient.

By subscribing to this theory of nutritionism, you are renouncing the intelligence of millions of years of evolution—millions of years of nature tweaking the recipe to ensure that organisms were getting the nutrition they needed, not only to survive but to thrive. Nature didn't design beta-carotene capsules; it designed a carrot. The context and delivery system, and all the interactions and interdependencies between individual food components are all relevant.

I liken it to having a beautiful engine in a car but no tires to get anywhere. For the body to absorb nutrients, you often need to have certain cofactors and symbiotic nutrients. For instance, you need ample fat to digest fat-soluble nutrients, like vitamin D. In other cases, there are nutrients that work better in tandems, such as B6 and magnesium. Studies have even shown cases where, once a nutrient is processed and delivered in supplement form, you no longer reap the benefits. In other situations, it may even be harmful; as seen in preliminary tests where beta-carotene increased the growth rate of skin tumors in mice[29].

Rather than place value on fruits, vegetables, and legumes, we now value products that are designed and processed from individual components, while claiming every benefit imaginable. Walk through your grocery store's processed-foods section. How many products make health claims? How many are fortified with calcium, fiber, omega-3s, or vitamin D? It's dizzying. You need a Ph.D. in biochemistry to pick out a healthy cereal. And with a marketing budget of over $30 billion annually, U.S. food companies will try to convince you of anything.

Instead of paying for how much it costs to grow and transport your food, you're paying for the convenience and apparent health value that comes from processing and fortification. I say apparent value because that is what it is, apparent. I often harp on the imperfect nature of nutritional science. There truly is no black and white, only gray. We don't have nanobots fused to proteins that follow the food as it is absorbed by our bodies. Instead, we have test subjects claiming that they ate this much of this food, at that time, in that proportion. Their information could be biased and inherently imperfect in nature. Even scientists and epidemiologists recognize the severe limitations of the studies they conduct. Health claims are weak at best. We need to become more aware. We need to scrutinize anything that makes a health claim, or better yet, not buy it.

I've been on the other side of the aisle as well. I have had arguments with marketers about taking the food out of food and replacing it with cheap garbage. These cases happened on more than one occasion. Here's a fact for you: companies out there are constantly trying to find new ways to take the 'good' parts of food out and replace them with cheap fillers that mimic the same nutritional profile. In the end, it's not food. It's a manufactured ingestible substance that has pseudo-nutritional benefits. Mmmmm, doesn't that sound tasty? I'll have seconds! Oh, and while you're at it, pass me that garbage on the street, as it probably has the same nutritional value as a typical box of cereal.

I can't remember the last time my broccoli had a health claim on it. If it did there definitely wouldn't be a package big enough to do justice to all its amazing benefits. Buy whole foods. Trust in nature. Keep it simple. Leave the turds for the birds.

Okay, Now What?

So when is it a good idea to look into supplementation? Well, the wrong answer is, "to compensate for a pathetic diet." I classify acceptable motivations for supplements into three distinct categories: inherent nutritional deficiencies in the food available, environmental influences, and focused performance or health benefit.

Since I've already touched on the nutritional state of our food, let's move onto environmental influences that would motivate supplement use. We grossly underestimate how the environmental impacts our health. People often take the myopic view of environmental impacts relating solely to pollution. I classify your environment as any 'noise' coming from your surroundings. While this list includes the obvious—exposure to toxins (pollutions) in our air, water, and food—it also encompasses stress, and improper sleep. Supplements can help deal with these 'uncontrollable' influences in our daily lives.

The last category—focused performance or health benefit—refers to supplementation to gain improvements in an area, regardless of diet. Some examples of this could be to improve athletic performance or to bolster energy and stamina.

For as long as vitamins have been around, there has been controversy over their effectiveness. A recent study by the non-profit Cochrane

Collaboration—an international network of over 28,000 people in 100 countries, who prepare the largest collection of randomized controlled trials in the world—sheds a little light on this misunderstood subject. It was shown that people, either healthy or sick, had little positive response to taking vitamins A, C, E, beta-carotene or selenium[30].

There are always several variables to consider, but this does shed light on the inadequacies of many processed vitamins, further supporting the flaws in reductionism. That is, it is not solely the effect of a micronutrient that is important, it is how it functions in relation to its whole food complement.

Society's prevailing attitude on nutrition is to take a multi-vitamin, often a futile endeavor. Again, over-processing takes what nature designed and reduces it to an unnatural form that the body hasn't been conditioned to ingest. Several studies have even shown that specific vitamin therapy may exacerbate breast and prostate cancers.

Vitamins should not be the answer to a poor diet. The answer to a poor diet is to improve it. I'm not saying that vitamins do not have their place. As whole food supplements, vitamins can be helpful at providing you with specific nutrients some people may otherwise be lacking. Vitamin D for northern dwellers is an example of a clear need and benefit.

Let's take a look at some of my favorite supplements whose nutrients are often difficult to obtain in our Western diet:

i. Omega-3

A typical North American diet includes only a fraction of what the World Health Organization recommends as being the minimum daily intake of omega-3. There are three types of omega-3 fatty acids, namely EPA, DHA, and ALA. Omega-3s are essential in that they are necessary for maintaining good health, but the body cannot produce them (i.e., EPA and DHA can be generated by the body if you have ALA present, but this is not optimal). Omega-3s are some of the most intensely studied supplements. Several claims substantiate that supplementing omega-3s is key to preventing several diseases and improving overall health, likely due to their anti-inflammatory benefits.

Here is a taste of the impressive resume of omega-3s, and why they draw so much attention. They can:

- reduce brain and cardiovascular inflammation
- improve cellular health, including skin health
- optimize fetal brain development
- support overall brain function, including mood
- improve glucose and insulin metabolism

Omega-3 fatty acids are typically found in marine (e.g., fish) and plant (e.g., flaxseed) oils. There are many excellent supplements out there. Try to find quality sources that are cold-processed and derived from wild, low -mercury sources.

ii. Vitamin D

For several years now vitamin D has been getting significant press for its cancer-fighting and anti-aging properties. There have been dozens of studies regarding recommended doses. Vitamin D has been shown to reduce chronic inflammation in the body, as well as ebb the deterioration of your DNA over time. It does this by inhibiting the body's inflammatory response. In doing so, turnover of cells is decreased, slowing the rate of DNA chromosome telomere deterioration—ostensibly slowing the aging process, and protecting against many diseases, such as cancer.

An efficient way to bolster your vitamin D stores is to get high-quality sun exposure. While we've been sold on how the sun can increase our risk of skin cancer, the chemicals in the majority of suntan lotions (e.g., oxybenzone and parabens) may arguably pose a greater risk. I'll discuss that in more detail in the section on *Toxins*.

We are being taught to fear the sun, yet the sun is the key to life on earth. Humans evolved to be in harmony with the sun. Our bodies need the sun. Yes, there are damaging UVB and UVA rays, however, in moderation, sun exposure can be healthy.

One little-known fact is that midday sun has the highest concentration of vitamin-D-inducing UVB rays. Midday is also when the sun is most intense. Start with limited exposure to ensure you do not burn—approximately 15-minutes—and slowly extend the time as your tolerance increases. If getting ample sun is not an option, there are high-quality vitamin D supplements derived from wild fish oils.

iii. Chlorella

Chlorella is a freshwater, single-celled algae loaded with vitamins, minerals, several trace elements, and is rich in chlorophyll. Chlorophyll has an amazing list of benefits:

- it optimizes oxygen delivery to your cells, through increased red blood cell production—more oxygen means more cellular energy
- through reducing inflammation, and supporting healthy bacteria growth in your intestines, it plays a huge role in bolstering your immune system

Chlorella delivers another crucial nutrient called iodine. Iodine is necessary for an efficiently functioning thyroid. The thyroid gland is critical for hormonal balance and operation. If your thyroid doesn't get the iodine it needs, your metabolism will suffer, and your energy levels will decrease. This energy lull partially explains why you often hear of weight gain associated with an improperly functioning thyroid.

Like most algae, chlorella is also an effective detoxifying agent, as it binds to heavy metals, and other toxins in the body. Next time you decide to drink more alcohol than you should, take chlorella to help avoid a hangover.

There are several different chlorella supplements on the market. Look for organic, broken-cell-wall chlorella—the cell wall of chlorella is not digestible, so it needs to be 'broken' to allow us to realize its full benefits.

iv. Resveratrol

Resveratrol is the active compound in red wine that has been getting accolades as of late. Recent studies have touted its anti-aging effects due to its impact on genes related to aging. Regardless of these potential effects, we know that it is a powerful antioxidant associated with:

- reduced risk of many cancers
- lower incidence of cardiovascular disease
- anti-aging

- bolstered immune system

v. Magnesium

Magnesium is the fourth most abundant element on earth. Magnesium ions are essential to all living things. Our bones and teeth contain approximately 65% percent of our magnesium, with our blood, fluids, and other body tissue housing the remaining percentage. It is essential for the functioning of hundreds of enzymes in your body, and also plays a key role in interacting with ATP (i.e., the energy 'currency' of our cells), RNA, and DNA. Since it cannot penetrate cell membranes, magnesium ions need to pair with transport proteins in supplemental form.

While magnesium is critical for our survival, it is estimated that over 50% of the population is deficient. This stat is alarming, in that, nerve and muscle function, bone health, and regulation of blood sugar all require magnesium. Also, caffeine, sugar, and alcohol promote the depletion of magnesium, while low acidity in the gut also decreases magnesium absorption.

Magnesium deficiency can lead to several diseases, including diabetes, anxiety disorders, and cardiovascular disease. If you eat a variety of nuts, fruits, and vegetables, you shouldn't need to take a magnesium supplement.

vi. CoQ10 (Ubiquinol)

CoQ10 is an essential vitamin used by every cell in your body. It is key to cellular respiration, and generates energy through ATP production. This process is responsible for approximately 95% of our energy. CoQ10 is instrumental in offsetting aging, in that it recycles other antioxidants, reducing DNA damage.

Deficiency in CoQ10 can cause heart failure, muscle weakness, fatigue, and premature aging. The older you become, the less efficient your body becomes at metabolizing CoQ10. Although found in several foods, its ubiquitous benefits in the body have made it one of the more popular supplements in the U.S. Taking a ubiquinol (i.e., fully broken down CoQ10) supplement will help offset the difficulty in metabolizing CoQ10 as you age. Moreover, if you are on statin drugs, it is advised to supplement CoQ10, as statins deplete CoQ10.

vii. Astaxanthin

Astaxanthin is an up-and-comer in a powerful class of antioxidants. It's a free-radical scavenging beast. It is believed by many to be the most potent carotenoid (i.e., an organic pigment found in plants). It is over 50x times more powerful than vitamin C and beta-carotene (another carotenoid), and over 10x more efficient than vitamin E at dealing with free radicals[31].

While other antioxidants can be overused, astaxanthin does not act as a pro-oxidant (i.e., causing oxidation), even in extremely high doses. Another interesting characteristic of this powerful antioxidant is that is soluble in both fat and water—meaning it can cross the blood-brain barrier, and assimilate in both fat and water in the body, allowing it penetrate and protect the entire cell. This solubility allows it to affect the brain and eyes, aiding in the protection of your nervous system and sight. Supplementation with astaxanthin can also act as an internal sunscreen. Some quality sources of this antioxidant are krill and other crustaceans.

viii. Vitamin B_{12}

B_{12}—often known as the energy vitamin—is a vital nutrient that we're finding increasingly difficult to obtain in the average diet. B_{12} has been shown to be effective at:
- repairing and maintaining a healthy nervous system
- supporting the immune system
- producing red blood cells
- sustaining energy levels
- maintaining cell growth and repair
- honing mental alertness
- converting carbohydrates and fatty acids into glucose (i.e., fuel)

B_{12} deficiency can be caused by ineffective absorption, or not obtaining sufficient amounts from your diet. It is especially difficult to absorb due to its physical size. Moreover, people with poor diets can over a period of time, significantly compromise their gut lining. This degradation of one's stomach lining is critical, in that parietal cells in the stomach lining produce hydrochloric acid and intrinsic factor—the vehicles for B_{12} absorption.

Apart from animal sources, there are virtually no other adequate sources of vitamin B_{12} (the B_{12} in spirulina is an analog and not effective). Even conventional red meat has decreasing levels of B_{12}, as Caged Animal Feed Operations (CAFOs) restrict any grazing that provides the animals B_{12} via the ingestion of grass and dirt.

In summary, it's becoming increasingly difficult to obtain B_{12} from a healthy diet. Virtually everyone could benefit from supplementing B_{12}. When taking a B-vitamin supplement it is important to take it within a whole-food complex, as high levels of one B vitamin can mask a deficiency in another (e.g., elevated levels of B6 can mask a deficiency in B_{12}).

There are fantastic organic, whole-food B-complex supplements on the market. We need approximately .4–2.8 micrograms of B_{12} daily, and a typical person can store 2–5 milligrams for months.

ix. Whey Protein

As explained earlier, protein is critical for several physiological processes. It is the building block for hormones, neurotransmitters, and antibodies, and is crucial for building healthy bones and muscles.

Whey protein is a common protein obtained from whey—a byproduct of dairy production. Whey protein has many benefits:

- readily assimilates in the body for efficient protein supply
- known as one of the best sources for obtaining the nutrients needed to produce glutathione (powerful antioxidant)
- instrumental in the formation of white blood cells, essential for overall immune responsiveness

Look for the following when sourcing a high-quality whey protein:

- whey isolates can be over-processed, so choose a micro-filtered source if possible (acid processing potentially denatures the amino acids), such as whey concentrate, which has a beneficial effect in stabilizing blood sugar
- whey typically contains lactose, so is not appropriate for those with lactose intolerance or a dairy sensitivity. There are lactose-free sources
- source it from hormone-free cows, which are grass fed, and

naturally raised. 100% New Zealand whey, preferably organic, is an excellent source
- it should be cold processed, as excessive heat may damage micronutrients
- avoid products that have artificial sweeteners
- whey should be free of toxic, heavy metals

x. Probiotics

I've explained the necessity of gut health and the importance of seeding good bacteria. Neither can be underestimated. The typical Western diet—plagued with high fructose corn syrup, antibiotics, lack of fiber, and overconsumption of dairy products—constantly bombards the lining of your gut, posing a significant threat to its health. Be proactive and help avoid the stresses on your gut, by loading up on soluble fiber (i.e., dissolves in the body), and plenty of fruits, vegetables, and legumes, which act as prebiotics—substances that promote the growth of healthy bacteria in the gastrointestinal tract.

As explained, the gut is estimated to be responsible for greater than 80% of your immune system. The health of your gut flora has a direct effect on your immune system, and the quality of your immune response to invaders. Once the lining of your gut is compromised, you may start absorbing improperly digested foods—'leaky gut'. This condition allows toxic substances (i.e., pathogenic bacteria and viruses flourish in an unhealthy gut) to enter the bloodstream, where some then bind to certain proteins, inciting an immune response. Symptoms of this condition may include depression, anxiety, rashes, or abdominal pain.

The key is to heal the damaged gut lining with fermented foods, and other probiotics. These probiotics represent the most efficient way to protect, and replenish, the good bacteria in your intestinal tract. Examples of fermented foods are sauerkraut, kimchi, and cultured dairy products. These cultured foods are also effective chelators—or detoxifiers—that help rid your body of heavy metals and other toxins.

While I recommend everyone include fermented foods in their diet, it is especially important for those with leaky gut. Just be sure to introduce them slowly, because if detoxification occurs too quickly, you can have a healing crisis, and experience flu-like symptoms. You can start a simple protocol, such as beginning with one teaspoon of fermented vegetables, wait a day or two, gauge your response and continue increasing the portions.

You can also buy probiotics off the shelf. There are hundreds of different options out there. Industry standards dictate that you should seek probiotics with at least 10^8–10^{10} CFU (colony-forming units) per day. CFU is a measure of the active bacterial content in a probiotic.

Eat Your Power Foods

Superfoods, or power foods, have become a hot topic. These foods are typically low calorie, yet very dense in nutrients and phytochemicals (i.e., plant chemicals). Blueberries or acai are some common examples.

Let's put the spotlight first on turmeric (a super-spice), followed by the rest of *Ikkuma's Top Eight Power Foods*.

Turmeric

For ages, in the Eastern hemisphere, turmeric has been known as a miracle spice. In the Western world, we are just beginning to understand the benefits of its active ingredient—curcumin. Curcumin is a potent anti-inflammatory agent—loaded with antioxidants—and has documented liver protection properties. It also has powerful immune boosting properties; having been shown to halt certain cancers, and prompt cancer cells to destroy themselves—a process called apoptosis. It does this through influencing dozens of pathways in the cell.

You need to start introducing this into your diet. Of all the power foods you'll find, turmeric is safe, and its cancer-fighting benefits are supported by extensive literature. Buy turmeric in your grocery store as a spice, or in health food stores as a supplement. Just make sure that it's certified organic, and free of fillers.

Ikkuma's Top 8 Power Foods

Power-Food	Benefits
Turmeric	• See previous page
Nettle	• Due to its high chlorophyll content, nettle is a good source of cellular energy • It is loaded with iron, and several other trace elements
Ginger	• Indian medicine recognizes ginger as the "universal remedy" • It is a potent anti-inflammatory, helps with nausea and boosts immunity
Cinnamon	• It boasts a newly discovered class of phytochemicals called chalcone polymers, which increase glucose metabolism in cells (i.e., blood sugar regulation) • Has been shown to lower blood pressure
Garlic	• This powerful antioxidant has been studied extensively for its wide range of health benefits • Anti-hypertensive, anti-microbial, anti-viral and anti-parasitic
Sauerkraut & Kimchi	• Effective at re-populating the gut with 'good' bacteria, improving immunity and digestion • Known to many as some of the healthiest foods, with all the properties of cabbage and more
Bee Pollen	• Incredibly nutritious with almost all known enzymes, minerals, trace elements, and amino acids • One of the few sources of B_{12}
Spirulina (micro-algae)—could also be considered a supplement like Chlorella	• Great detoxifier—cell walls bind to heavy metals • High in protein, Omega-3s, and 9 amino acids—unfortunately the B_{12} is an 'analogue' which does not provide the benefits of the B_{12} you find in meats

Alkaline Versus Acidic Foods... WTF? (What's the Fuss?)

Our bodies are a chemical laboratory. One of the indicators of our chemical balance, pH, is the measurement of the acidity and alkalinity of a solution. Our bodies work most efficiently at a pH around 7.4, which is slightly alkaline (7 is neutral). If our pH is consistently below 7—a state of acidosis (i.e., an acidic environment)—chronic inflammation can occur. As we have learned, chronic inflammation can lead to many degenerative diseases, such as cancer, and osteoporosis.

An acidic environment in the body results in leaching of alkalizing minerals from the largest reserve in our body—the bones. Minerals from the bones are used to buffer our blood's acidity, and excess minerals end being deposited into tissues. Interestingly enough, the Western world consumes the highest amounts of dairy, yet we have some of the highest rates of osteoporosis. This seeming paradox is an example of an acidity issue, not a lack of calcium issue.

In the next major section of the book, we will discuss potentially unhealthy foods in detail. Many of the foods we will discuss are also foods that promote an acidic environment or are acid forming within the body, such as sugar, refined grains, meat, coffee, and alcohol. Don't get confused with the actual pH of some foods and their effects in the body. Although lemon has a relatively low pH—well under 7—it has powerful alkalizing implications in the body.

Acidic Forming and Alkalizing Foods

More acidic	Less Acidic	Types of Food	Less Alkaline	More Alkaline
Navy beans, pinto beans	Cooked spinach, kidney beans, string beans	Vegetables & Beans	Peas, carrots, tomatoes, cabbage, olives, mushrooms	Onions, raw spinach, broccoli, vegetable juices, garlic
Blackberries, cranberries	Oranges, processed fruit juices, plums	Fruits	Bananas, pineapple, peaches, avocados	Lemon, lime, grapefruit, watermelon
Artificial sweeteners	Refined sugar, molasses	Sweeteners	Raw honey, maple syrup	Stevia
White flour, pasta, white rice	Wheat, brown rice, spelt	Grains	Amaranth, quinoa, wild rice	
Peanuts, walnuts	Sunflower seeds, pumpkin seeds	Nuts & Seeds	Chestnuts	Almonds
	Corn oil	Oils	Canola oil	Olive oil

		Meats		
Beef, pork, shellfish	Turkey, chicken, cold-water fish			
Cheese, homogenized milk, ice cream	Eggs, yogurt, cottage cheese	**Eggs & Dairy**	Whey, Goat cheese, goat milk	
Alcohol, soft drinks	Coffee, tea	**Beverages**	Green tea	Herbal teas, lemon water

From www.phreshproducts.com

While there are also healthy foods that can be acid-forming, it is the amount consumed that determines the effect they will have in the body. The key is to balance acidic foods with eating high quality, organic, alkalizing foods, such as kale, raw spinach, almonds, and avocados. Fresh vegetable juices, greens powders, such as chlorella and spirulina, and lemon water taken between meals, are great ways to alkalize your body. A good practice to follow would be to eat alkalizing foods for 65%–80% of your diet, with the remaining one-third being quality acidic foods, such as eggs, and lean meats.

Before wrapping up the *Foods To 'Live' By* section, I'd like to stress that our bodies have evolved over thousands of years, and this evolution happened in concert with the foods available. Our bodies crave real food. When you are eating chemically altered and overly processed industrial food, you are essentially eating dead food. Your body needs nutrients, which it cannot effectively get from manufactured foods. Dependence on sugars and processed food is literally like a drug addiction. It may be tough at first to improve your diet, but within days your body will start to repair itself, and within weeks your addiction to modern processed food will fade.

Ikkuma INFO: TYPICAL DAY OF EATING AND SNACK IDEAS

Now that you are armed with a wealth of information regarding what you should be eating, here is what I would consider a healthy day in the life of a SuperHuman-inspired eater:

Morning: Wake up to a filtered glass of water containing the juice from half a lemon. Immediately drink another glass of water to further hydrate and wash the acid from your teeth. Wait about 30–45 minutes for your metabolism to kick-start, then prepare an *Ikkuma 'SuperHuman' Smoothie* (see recipe earlier in the section).

Mid-Morning: If you start to get hunger pangs before lunch, what you need is some healthy protein, fiber, and fats to cut your cravings. The following are some great snacks:

• Celery stalks w/ almond butter and raisins	• Carrots with hummus
• Apple with a handful of almonds (raw or roasted)	• Kale chips
• Organic yogurt (source coconut yogurt if you're lactose deficient), and organic blueberries	• Left over vegetables, and chicken or fish from the night before
• Various berries (which are low sugar and high fiber)	NOTE: you can't eat junk food if it isn't in your house, so don't have it around

Lunch: A good option would be a salad, with a variety of greens and other healthy fruits and vegetables, topped off with pastured chicken or wild Alaskan salmon. This can be seasoned with balsamic vinaigrette. Quinoa can also be a great addition to a salad.

Mid-Afternoon: Always pay attention to drinking water throughout the day. You want to avoid water consumption within 30-minutes of a meal. Water consumption during a meal rushes the digestion process and dilutes critical stomach acids, sabotaging proper digestion. When the need strikes to have a snack in the afternoon, the choices listed for mid-morning are excellent choices at this time of day as well.

Dinner: Ideally, dinner would be eaten at around 6pm, to allow the liver to recover during your sleep. Eating too late in the evening does not allow your liver to get much of a break—after digesting dinner—before it has to get back to work in the morning. A reasonable dinner could consist of some pastured chicken or fish, coupled with a variety of brightly-colored vegetables. Starches, such as potatoes, should be limited late in the day. Sweet potatoes or wild brown rice in moderation would be fine for an early dinner.

Ikkuma Top *Foods To 'Live' By* Tweets:

- Many of us walk around chronically dehydrated. **Water** is the first step to getting healthy. Find pure sources, or use reverse osmosis.
- **Eggs** are a nearly-perfect protein and high in beta-carotene (i.e., keep eyes healthy). Pastured eggs are best. http://bit.ly/13UyB3R
- **Avoid harmful antibiotics and hormones.** Choose organically raised meats. They may also have higher levels of (critical vitamin) B_{12}.
- **Load up on green, leafy vegetables.** They are cancer-fighters, and packed with antioxidants designed to reduce chronic inflammation in the body.
- **Make breakfast smart.** Load up on low-glycemic, high-fiber foods. My morning *Ikkuma 'SuperHuman' Smoothie* is a great kick-start to the day.
- **Eat a broad range of colors.** Colorful fruits and vegetables are loaded with flavonoids (i.e., powerful antioxidants). The darker, the better.
- **Stick to high-fiber complex carbs,** like vegetables and whole grains. This high-quality fiber helps control the rate of sugar absorption.
- Smaller fish like sardines and krill are loaded with heart-healthy omega-3s. Ensure supplements are high quality. http://bit.ly/11ukq8m
- **Snack on nuts.** Jammed with healthy omega-3s and -6s, nuts also curb your appetite before a meal. Buy raw nuts, then lightly roast.
- **Eat while you are relaxed, and take your time.** Being relaxed will optimize digestion. Digestion begins in the mouth, so chew your food well.
- **Avoid drinking liquids within 30-minutes of a meal.** Liquids dilute your digestive juices and can lead to gastric reflux, gas, and bloating.
- **Eat simple meals.** Avoid eating large amounts of food in one sitting. It slows digestion, which can lead to indigestion and fatigue.
- **Eat fruit on its own, between meals.** Fruit digests very quickly and can ferment if eaten after a large meal, leading to gas and bloating.
- **Organic** is simply better for you and the environment. Fewer pesticides and chemicals in your food can't be bad. http://bit.ly/18CsgwW

- **Steer clear of GMOs.** GMOs are not effectively tested, and their properties are potentially harmful. http://bit.ly/17fWRBr
- **Vitamin D** is a supreme cancer fighter. Embrace the sun in moderation for the best-source nature has to offer.
- **Go green.** Chlorella is an algae efficient at detoxification and ultra-rich in nutrients. Don't forget that they are great for hangovers.
- **Magnesium is critical.** Deficiency can lead to several diseases. Get it from a variety of dark fruits and vegetables, and nuts and seeds.
- Every cell in the body uses the 'energy' **vitamin CoQ10.** It has important anti-aging properties. We need more as we age.
- **Vitamin B$_{12}$**—king of the B vitamins, yet the most elusive—factors in cell growth and repair. Organic meats are good sources.
- Upwards of 80% of your immune system lies in your gut. **Probiotics** keep the gut healthy. Fermented foods and yogurt are excellent sources.
- **Turmeric** needs to be part of your diet. It's a miracle Indian spice that you can find almost anywhere and fights cancer like none other.
- **Load up on alkaline foods.** An acidic environment in the body leads to inflammation and disease. Here are some choices: http://bit.ly/18E8AJ3
- **Throw away junk food.** You can't eat what you don't have. Stockpile healthy and delicious protein, and fiber-loaded, foods.

Bonus Ikkuma *Foods To 'Live' By* Tweets:

- **Drink organic green tea.** Its potent polyphenols help protect your heart and fight cancer.
- **Coffee in moderation can be healthy.** It is a bitter herb that helps detoxify the body, and has healthy antioxidants. A light roast is best.
- **Olive oil and cooking don't mix.** A better cooking option, coconut oil, has a higher burning point. It's best to eat olive oil raw.
- **Eat whole foods.** When foods are processed and refined, nutrients are removed from the food, and left out or reintroduced ineffectively.

Part **TWO**
Foods To 'Drive By'

(*Ikkuma Translation: The Fire Is Starting to Fade*)

> *"Preserving health by too severe a rule is a worrisome malady."*
> —Francois Duc de la Rochefoucauld,
>   17th century French author

"Are you kidding me?" That was my first reaction when someone I was coaching said she didn't want to give up pizza because she liked it. I couldn't believe what I was hearing. Don't get me wrong. I like pizza. And since I have done the work, and maintained a healthy lifestyle, I can afford to indulge now and then. So, based on that logic, having pizza is one withdrawal I can make. But if you haven't done the work, then sorry, you need to skip that pizza—at least until you get your health on track.

The advice in this section should be easy to abide by because all you need to do is avoid eating crap that's not good for you. That's it. No sit-ups. No marathons. Just avoid crap. Avoid the crap we invented 50 years ago to increase corporate profits. Avoid the crap not even fit for rats.

If you're serious about getting healthy, the nuggets in this section are a must. To make it even easier, I'll give you a piece of advice that will change your life forever. Just don't have junk food in your kitchen. If it's not there, you can't eat it. Simple, right?

You don't think after a long night out I wouldn't be tempted to eat a bowl of greasy, salty chips? Of course I would. After a couple of cocktails, the short-term satisfaction of so-called comfort foods can easily seduce yours truly.

While we can't constantly stress about eating perfect, there are some foods that you should always avoid. In this section, I'll elaborate, and encourage you to consider eliminating these foods from your diet. The key is to make the transition to optimal health manageable within the framework of your already hectic life.

At first, you may make excuses as to why you can't eliminate or cut down on a particular food. Try to make it easier on yourself by having short-term milestones. Your body will eventually wean itself off these harmful foods, and reward you for it.

Before I move on, I want to once again shine a light on our global obsession with processed foods. Here are some startling facts, as reported in a December 2012 issue of *The Economist*:

- 25 million Americans visit McDonald's every day
- during the past decade alone, sales of packaged foods have risen by 92%. Soft drink sales have doubled over the same period
- in India, Brazil, and China, the numbers are even scarier, with soft drinks sales increasing by 400% over the past decade

Nearly every processed food contains refined grains, sugars, additives, artificial colors, and flavors—all of which harm your health. Sadly, in the face of the obesity epidemic, at a time when we should be improving our dietary habits, we are digressing at an exponential rate. So let's get started and take a look at some of the food dangers out there.

Key Foods to Avoid

i. Modern Wheat Products

Estimates are that wheat has been around for at least 12,000 years. With the advent of wheat, ancient civilizations were able to thrive, as it was easy to cultivate, and it could be stored for times of need. If the wheat we eat today was anywhere near the structure of ancient wheat, then it may have been spared from this section.

Over thousands of years, wheat has undergone tens of thousands of hybridizations. These alterations have structurally mutated the wheat, with increased levels of gluten a noticeable byproduct. Gluten is inherently difficult to digest, and is responsible for various autoimmune conditions, including celiac disease.

Modern wheat's protein content is another result of its evolution. Modern wheat is typically about 15% protein—that's approximately half the percentage of ancient strains. Unfortunately, ancient strains of wheat are next to impossible to find.

The issues don't end there. Some researchers conclude that upwards of 5% of the proteins of wheat hybrids are unique (i.e., not present in either of the parents). These unpredictable genetic arrangements may change its protein structure, thus affecting organs in unknown ways. In effect, our bodies are dealing with them for the first time. GMOs create similarly novel proteins. There is no real good news here. Decades of hybridized wheat have resulted in new strains that our bodies may find difficult to process.

Modern wheat also has higher levels of Amylopectin-A, which is very easy to digest, spiking our blood sugar. Conversely, legumes, like beans, contain Amylopectin B and C, not as easily digestible.

Now, you may think that you're making a healthy choice by opting for whole-wheat bread, but it's so over-processed and refined that it spikes your blood sugar similar to white bread. To put this into perspective, two slices of whole wheat bread raises blood sugar much like a can of soda pop, or a chocolate bar. This blood sugar high typically lasts about two hours before the crash hits. And this isn't just a sugar high. The polypeptides from wheat, and other carbohydrates, have been shown to bind to opiate receptors—meaning wheat has a potentially neurological or addictive effect, fuelled by the release of serotonin.

Another comfort food, pasta, spikes blood sugar for four–six hours (depending on the variety), with whole-wheat pasta having a marginally muted impact. The reason for the difference in sugar absorption rate is because we metabolize pasta differently than bread. So although you may be consuming a similar amount of carbs, they get absorbed at different rates.

Never neglect the detriments that increased blood sugar can have on the body. Remember the vicious cycle: excess glucose—high blood sugar—insulin response—fat—insulin resistance—diabetes. One of the more noticeable results of this death spiral is visceral fat. It's unfortunate that what was once such a reliable food staple has been mutated into something that contributes to excess weight and health issues.

Now back to gluten. As mentioned, gluten is a notoriously problematic protein found in wheat, rye, and other grains. The lectins in wheat, which are rich in proline—a non-essential amino acid—can also cause potential damage to your gut. The issues caused by gluten and lectins are quite similar, in that they both affect the body's immune system, and—similar to dairy proteins—are both difficult for your body to digest.

Once damaged by poor diet, our intestinal wall may allow some of these undigested proteins to enter the bloodstream. For many people, their body mistakes these proteins for foreign invaders, prompting an immune response. This immune response will, at a minimum, cause gut irritation and inflammation, which, as explained earlier, can lead to a leaky gut. A leaky gut is the gateway to several autoimmune diseases, such as Type-I Diabetes, celiac disease, and multiple sclerosis.

Things start to get very troubling when the foreign invaders resemble healthy proteins in the body. In some cases, the antibodies will attack healthy cells, such as pancreatic beta cells, thus compromising the pancreas.

Gluten also affects the functioning of glutaminase, which has a hand in modifying every protein in our body—meaning that it has the potential to affect any organ.

It's important to moderate your consumption of all grains, ensuring the ones you do eat are whole grains, and ideally gluten-free (e.g., millet, quinoa, amaranth). No matter what you choose, ensure that it is organically grown, and always non-GMO. There are many products available, from pasta to bread, that are now using gluten-free grains, thanks to the rise of gluten intolerance.

It is also important to keep in mind that just because products may be 'gluten-free', it doesn't mean there are no consequences to overindulging. In most cases, gluten is replaced with refined carbs, such as rice starch and tapioca starch (both are gluten-free, but are refined carbs), which may as well be table sugar.

ii. Dairy

Dairy is a hot topic in nutritional circles. Some believe it's critical for maintaining healthy bones and calcium intake, while others believe that it's detrimental to our health and should be avoided. Despite our differences of opinion, we were all raised believing that we should eat according to the four food groups and their associated serving recommendations, with dairy being one of these four food groups.

A sad reality is that there were a lot of political motivations for promoting these four food groups. This is a nice way of saying that powerful lobbyists influenced policy. So once again it's incumbent upon us to do our own due diligence, and make food decisions for ourselves.

Let's dismiss opinion and analyze the facts. Dairy contains lactose (i.e., milk sugars), and milk fats that are often difficult to for our bodies to digest. Our bodies need lactase to break down lactose, however as we age, our body's production of lactase decreases, by upwards of 90%. Ineffective processing of lactose can create an acidic environment in the body; fertile ground for the growth of harmful bacteria.

The liver needs to secrete a type of bile high in sulfur to metabolize milk fats. Some harmful bacteria thrive in this environment, causing havoc in the gastrointestinal tract, potentially breaking down the mucosal barrier—which protects the stomach from its powerful acids. Adding to this is the body's subsequent immune response to these poorly digested fats. This immune response may create even more damage to this delicate system. Remember that the billions of friendly bacteria in our gut are our first protection against deadly pathogens. Compromising this environment can lead to a host of immune disorders.

It gets worse. Dairy contains casein protein. In animal studies, casein protein consumption above the 10% RDA correlated with exponential growth of foci—cancer precursor cells. It has been shown to act as fuel for tumors[1].

Even if you think dairy is good for you, the romanticized images of dairy production are a thing of the past. Cows are part of a manufacturing process where the majority of them are raised in Caged Animal Feed Operations (CAFOs). In these 'factories', cows are often confined to small feedlots where they show severe signs of stress due to social isolation, and are incapable of moving around or even laying down.

Conversely, since the 2010 final ruling by the USDA[2], USDA Organic Certified farms are required to give cows access to pasture. As of 2008, less than 1% of all farms in the U.S. were managed organically compared to over 4% in Europe[3].

Within these CAFOs—to optimize milk production—operators can employ several techniques, including antibiotic and growth hormone (e.g., rBGH in the U.S.) usage, and over-milking. There are predictable complications with such an aggressive push for production. The cows often become sick and develop infections, which are then treated with even more chemicals. Despite safeguards, some studies have found several different chemicals in our milk, including highly toxic compounds such as PCDDs (a dioxin), and dioxin-like compounds, along with puss, pathogens, and blood from various infections[4]. Thus amplifying the need to pasteurize milk before packaging. Pasteurization, along with killing good bacteria, compromises some of the nutritional value of the milk.

If you need or want to continue consuming milk, it would be best to buy from a Certified Organic dairy farmer. As another alternative, organic goat or sheep's milk is often better tolerated by people with dairy sensitivities. The best option would be to seek out organic coconut or almond milk.

Ikkuma INFO: RECOMBINANT BOVINE GROWTH HORMONE

This growth hormone is a synthetic version of a hormone produced naturally by the cow's pituitary glands. Its primary purpose is to increase the cow's milk production. Although Canada, the EU, and several other countries banned rBGH, it's injected in nearly a third of all cows in the U.S. Once again the U.S. trails the rest of the world in protecting its citizens. Moreover, the milk produced from these cows has elevated levels of the hormone IGF-1. This hormone messes with your pituitary glands, having adverse effects on your metabolic and hormonal balance. In excess, IGF-1 is correlated with higher rates of many cancers[5].

iii. Sugar and Fructose

Let's review some startling facts about sugar:

- Americans consume over ninety pounds of sugar annually, on top of what they consume naturally from fruits and vegetables. This is well over the amount needed to cause metabolic dysfunction[6]
- In the American Heart Association journal *Circulation*, a study following approximately 43,000 men for over twenty years reported that consuming one 12-ounce sweetened beverage per day would increase the likelihood of a heart attack by 20%

These are just two of the hundreds of jaw-dropping stats related to sugar consumption in the Western world. Sugar consumption is indeed out of control.

Sugar (sucrose) is composed of equal parts glucose and fructose. When you consume sugar, the pancreas produces insulin to shuttle the sugar where it is needed, namely your muscles and your brain. Your liver then metabolizes the remaining sugar, either storing it or producing fatty acids (which are subsequently stored as fat). When you consume sugar in excess, the cells in your body become increasingly insulin resistant due to a myriad of factors, one being fatty acid overload. The pancreas then needs to work harder to produce more insulin. When insulin resistance reaches critical levels, the stage is set for Type-II Diabetes.

Leptin is another hormone affected by excess sugar consumption. Excessive sugar consumption decreases leptin sensitivity. Leptin helps manage your hunger. When leptin sensitivity decreases, the signal to stop eating is weakened, leading to even more overconsumption.

This detrimental pattern leads to obesity and other related diseases, such as metabolic syndrome. Metabolic syndrome is a combination of risk factors—insulin resistance, elevated cholesterol, and high blood pressure (i.e., hypertension)—that increase the probability of diseases such as cardiovascular disease (CVD), stroke, and diabetes. It is caused by overall metabolic dysfunction and is fuelled by unhealthy habits, such as excessive sugar consumption.

Ikkuma INFO: SUPRISING SUGAR LEVELS IN COMMON FOODS

We need to be very wary of many of the foods we eat, in that they may have high amounts of sugar. Keep in mind that a safe level of added sugar for the average consumer is approximately 25 grams per day. Here are some foods that have sugar levels comparable to a candy bar:

- Canned Fruit: we need to consume fruit in moderation. Canned fruit is a bigger issue. It often contains syrup that is loaded with sugar. Some products contain over 30 grams of sugar
- Tomato Sauce: this seemingly healthy food, packed with cancer-fighting lycopene, often has added sugar. This added sugar, as well as the pasta it's typically eaten with, can create a significant sugar spike

- Fat-Free Salad Dressing: often times, fats are replaced with fillers such as sugars and starches. Healthy fat is not evil. Carbs are a bigger concern for obesity and chronic disease
- Yogurt: many yogurts have added sugar or artificial sweeteners (which I will discuss shortly). They often contain artificial colors and flavors. Look for unsweetened, or naturally sweetened, organic, full-fat yogurts. As you now know, fat-free is often full of replacement sugars
- Muffins: even bran muffins almost always contain a significant amount of sugar to make them tastier. Muffins are primarily carbs, often packing well over 30 grams of sugar
- Granola bars: we often consider granola to be a healthy snack. The sad truth is that most granola bars have sugar as the #1 ingredient. Even the granola itself is a potent carbohydrate, in that it eventually gets metabolized into sugar

One type of sweetener that we need to be keenly aware of is high-fructose corn syrup (HFCS). You can find high-fructose corn syrup in a significant percentage of the processed food at the supermarket.

Corn—highly subsidized in the U.S.—is artificially inexpensive, resulting in corn-based sweeteners as the sweeteners of choice for food processors. A lot of businesses are constantly looking for cheap fillers to put in their food. High fructose corn syrup is the 'cheap-filler' king, so companies love it.

Every cell in your body uses glucose, with typically about 20% metabolized by your liver. Whereas the liver needs to metabolize nearly 100% of the fructose you consume, because it alone is equipped to handle it—in a process called fructolysis. Hence, when we consume HFCS in excess, fructose can overtax the liver, damaging it much like excessive alcohol consumption. This process can lead to non-alcoholic fatty liver disease (NAFLD), which, terrifyingly enough, is starting to affect our children[7].

It is important to understand how fructose affects our bodies, and how it's metabolized in the body. Research shows that fructose helps deplete the energy of a cell, preventing it from functioning normally, causing oxidative stress, and inflammation. Fructose is also responsible for creating advanced glycation enzymes (AGEs), which accelerate the aging process.

Some theorize that fructose promotes obesity, not due to the calories it provides, but due to a unique physiological response in the body. Fructose activates a key enzyme, fructokinase, which in turn activates another enzyme that promotes fat accumulation in cells. You could liken fructose to a fat storage switch.

In essence, fructose sabotages your appetite management system. It doesn't adequately stimulate insulin production, resulting in a state where the body does not suppress your hunger hormone (i.e., ghrelin), yet suppresses the satiety hormone (i.e., leptin). This suppression double-whammy has a dangerous domino effect, as the increase in appetite will prompt a person to eat more, which in turn can lead to insulin resistance, metabolic syndrome, and potentially Type-2 Diabetes and heart disease.

Research has found similarities between metabolic syndrome in humans, and the metabolism of hibernating mammals. These animals have fat storage conditions; with all the same symptoms of metabolic syndrome—fatty liver, increased triglycerides, and insulin resistance. Studies in rats have also shown that fructose promoted a metabolic-syndrome-type condition that did not appear in rats that were fed glucose.

Fructose in its whole food form (i.e., apple vs. apple juice) is less of a shock to your body because fruit contains other macronutrients, such as fiber, that slow the entry of fructose into the bloodstream. Again, fructose outside of whole food, such as high-fructose corn syrup, is the true culprit.

Ikkuma INFO: TOXIC EFFECT OF FRUCTOSE

Fructose and alcohol affect the liver in many similar ways. Since the liver metabolizes nearly 100% of the fructose you consume, fructose can overload the liver much like excessive alcohol. They have very similar toxic effects, namely visceral fat, fatty liver, metabolic syndrome, and insulin resistance. Fructose is also believed to stimulate the pleasure centers of the brain, encouraging people to over-consume, much like a narcotic. Like alcohol, we need to control our fructose consumption.

So remember, a calorie is not always a calorie. All calories are not made equal. One significant difference between consumption of fructose versus glucose, protein, or fats is the hormonal response they elicit. Even if you consume the same number of calories from each, they will have very different effects on how much fat you accumulate. Remember—except for post-workout, or fasting-induced glycogen depletion—that nearly 100% of the fructose you consume gets metabolized by your liver. Fructose is also several times more reactive than glucose in producing advanced glycation end products, which accelerate the aging process. Remember, glucose and fructose are very different animals.

iv. Artificial Sweeteners

If high-fructose corn syrup is the cheap-filler king, then artificial sweeteners are the evil prince. At least with HFCS you know what you're getting. Artificial sweeteners, on the other hand, are a more complex animal. While believed to help with weight management, they can induce carb cravings, stimulate appetite, and promote weight gain (fat storage). The various types of sweeteners—aspartame (e.g., Equal), sucralose (e.g., Splenda), and acesulfame potassium (e.g., Acesulfame-K)—have various claims against them, from causing neurological damage to having carcinogenic properties, and wreaking havoc on gut health. I have a hard time keeping my food down if I mistakenly consume artificial sweeteners. After this section you may feel the same.

Though there are several artificial sweeteners available, let's focus our attention toward the two most popular: aspartame and sucralose.

Aspartame has a sullied history of which few are aware. It took several votes in the early 80s for the FDA to somehow approve aspartame as fit for use. It was initially approved in the early 70's and subsequently overturned. As Dr. Mercola explains in *"Artificial Sweeteners: More Sour Than You Ever Imagined"*[8] aspartame has been linked to several adverse effects such as seizures, nausea, and anxiety attacks. The main components of aspartame are the chemicals phenylalanine, aspartic acid, and methanol—all causing potential havoc in the human body:

- an abundance of phenylalanine in your brain can decrease serotonin levels, causing mood disorders

- excess aspartic acid can destroy neurons, by allowing excess calcium to penetrate your cells
- the oxidation of methanol inside the body creates toxins, such as formaldehyde, which are toxic and carcinogenic

Even moderate consumption of aspartame introduces levels of methanol in the body well above the EPA recommended dosage[9].

Although we find both phenylalanine and aspartic acid in many proteins (in proper combinations with other amino acids), when consumed as isolated amino acids they are no longer inert and become harmful. As reported by the FDA, aspartame is responsible for more reports of adverse reactions than all other food and food additives combined.

Next on the list is sucralose, which was approved by the FDA in 1998. In animal studies, this sweetener has been shown to severely reduce—by upwards of 50%—the amount of good bacteria in the gut and digestive tract, and contribute to increases in body weight[10]. It's an unnatural sweetener that veils itself as an alternative to sugar. You should never use sucralose as an alternative to sugar.

When we consume, artificially sweetened, no-calorie foods, they increase our craving for more carbohydrate-rich foods. Remember that sugars are carbohydrates, and carbohydrates are the body's fuel. We have a hunger for carbohydrates for a reason... energy. Our brains have been hardwired to expect calories when they encounter sweetness, and when this caloric reward does not occur, it craves that void to be filled. While we think that consuming sugar-free sweets helps us lose weight, in actuality, they increase our cravings for more full-calorie carbohydrates.

Artificial sweeteners are not necessary, and are easy to phase out of your diet. Pay particular attention to anything sugar-free because if it's sweet, chances are it contains artificial sweeteners. Better alternatives to artificial sweeteners are organic stevia or pure dextrose.

v. Alcohol

"The problem with some people is that when they aren't drunk, they're sober."
—W.B. Yeats, Irish poet

"First you take a drink, then the drink takes a drink, then the drinks takes you."
—F. Scott Fitzgerald, American novelist

I've been known to enjoy a well-mixed cocktail. But I do have my limits and know them well, and for the most part, I abide by them.

Alcohol is not all bad. In moderation, it has been shown to help reduce hypertension, increase good cholesterol (HDL), reduce the formation of blood clots, and potentially help prevent arterial damage caused by bad cholesterol (LDL).

Alcohol in moderation means different things to different people. Doing belly shots after polishing off a bottle is not moderation. Moderation looks more like a couple of drinks a day for men, and one for women. In these quantities, you reap the beneficial effects of alcohol, regardless of the alcohol you choose. The difference in recommended amounts lies in the fact that men usually weigh more, and are physiologically better equipped to metabolize alcohol.

Some swear by red wine due to its health benefits (namely, resveratrol content), but as reported by the Mayo Clinic (*Red Wine and Resveratrol: Good for Your Heart?*), you would need to drink over sixty liters of wine in one sitting to mimic the amounts of resveratrol shown to have beneficial effects in mice studies.

Take note—there are still risk factors to drinking daily, including increased cancer risk. If you continually abuse alcohol, you can severely compromise your liver, lose water-soluble vitamins (specifically B vitamins), and reduce insulin's effectiveness—much like the effect of a poor diet. New news this is not.

Alcohol consumption can become habit forming, so I'm not advocating for people to start drinking to improve their health. But, if you do enjoy the odd drink, it may be helping you in the long run.

vi. Trans Fats (or Trans Fatty Acids)

Humanmade trans fats have been around for over fifty years. Remember all those cookies and cakes we ate growing up? They probably had an unhealthy helping of trans fats. Trans fats are (typically) superheated polyunsaturated corn, or soy, oils with added hydrogen. They have the resilience of saturated fats, in that they are stable in processed foods over long periods of time, yet wreak havoc on the liver in several ways.

As we definitively learned in the 1990's, trans fats are indeed an incredibly destructive invention. They have been linked to several debilitating conditions, such as cancer and hormonal imbalances. They have also been found to increase LDL cholesterol and lower HDL cholesterol, enhancing the risk of heart disease[10]. There are some arguments that trans fats are no worse that saturated fats, however a study conducted in 2004, reported in Atherosclerosis, Thrombosis and Vascular Biology, illustrated that trans fats had a more detrimental effect on heart-healthy HDL cholesterol than saturated fats.

The government now strictly controls trans fats, including requiring labeling in processed foods, making it easier to eliminate them from your diet. In places like New York City, trans fats are banned from restaurants. This is a long-overdue step in the right direction.

We Have a Choice

At this point in the book I can't help but reflect on the food processing inventions of the past several decades. It's important that everyone takes the time to reflect on the advent of food processing, and mechanically engineered food products.

Ask yourself if manufactured food has improved the quality of your health. I believe that when you become aware of how these refined, manufactured, and processed foods react in your body, and the correlations between them and increased incidences of disease, you'll choose to cut them out of your diets.

Furthermore, despite being known to cause severe damage to public health, the companies responsible for these pseudo-nutritional foods continue to come across as if they are designing products to improve our health, and increase the availability of quality food. Yet, for most multinationals, their sole interest lies in financial gain. The food industry, along with government regulators, should be ashamed at what they've unleashed on the general public in the past fifty years.

We are experimental rats in financially lucrative laboratory experiments. There was nothing wrong with food choices in the early 1900's, if indeed you had a choice. While our ancestors did not have access to the variety of whole foods we now have, nearly everything they ate was grown, not processed. Most jobs were in farming. Life was slower.

The answers are simple. The question is: what are you willing to sacrifice to create the healthy body you want? Are you prepared to go with one less electronic gadget, or spend that extra 15 minutes to prepare a proper meal instead of an instant dinner? These are not choices I can make for you. However, I hope you now feel equipped to choose better.

Stop deluding yourself into thinking that you'll get away with questionable lifestyle decisions in the long run. The Canadian Cancer Society predicts that, on average, we'll spend the last ten years of our lives battling a disease. Go to your nearest hospital and see if you like the ambiance. If you're going to be sick for ten years, you'd better get used to it. Better yet, ask some chronic disease sufferers what they think. It's time to stop the cycle of ignorance and make changes.

Ikkuma Top *Foods To 'Drive' By* Tweets:

- **Wheat** has undergone several changes over time. It's high in gluten (an issue for many), and often overly processed. Choose healthier grains.
- **Milk**—a diet staple for years—is difficult for the body to metabolize, and is acidic in nature. Vegetables are excellent calcium alternatives.
- In the U.S., **rBGH** (a hormone that increases milk production, and is known to be harmful) is still legal for use in cattle. Avoid it. http://huff.to/13P2SRE
- **High-fructose corn syrup** is linked to rampant obesity. Nearly 100% of fructose consumed directly hits the liver. Nuff said. http://huff.to/17UEjo7

- Many apparently healthy foods have **loads of sugar**. Read the label and make smart choices. Some high-sugar foods will shock you. http://bit.ly/17UEP5y
- To **combat fat gain** from processed and sugary foods, try intermittent fasting. See my *Ikkuma Info: Intermittent Fasting*.
- **Ditch the artificial sweeteners**. Don't be fooled by their zero calorie claims. They're toxic, and induce overeating. http://bit.ly/13ptGsh
- **Alcohol in moderation**—1 to 2 drinks per day—can be beneficial. Yet, binge drinking can be very toxic to your liver, and is highly acidic.
- **Avoid trans fats,** or any other food with hydrogenated on the label. They tax your heart, and lead to weight gain. http://mayocl.in/16OtPG6
- **Avoid foods with health claims**. Selling us on fortified foods is just another gimmick to sell fake nutrition. Real food doesn't need a health claim.
- **Beware of 'natural flavoring.'** It often disguises the presence of MSG, which induces your brain to eat more. http://bit.ly/1224VPW

Section
THREE

Toxins...
The Ugly Truth

(Ikkuma Translation: 'Get That Tire Out of the Fire!')

"Learn to live in balance—When we open our eyes to the underlying wholeness of life, our actions will shift. Nature will again become our partner in the creation of a conscious healthy world."—S. LeBlanc

"Our own physical body possesses a wisdom which we who inhabit the body lack. We give it orders which make no sense."
—Henry Miller, American Author

In talking about organics earlier in the book, you were sensitized to the ubiquity of toxins, and their far-reaching effects on humans and the environment. This quick overview framed up what we'll now dive into in more detail. The end in mind for this section is for you to gain insight on the toxic dangers out there, and feel confident that there are options.

I'd like to start the discussion by putting the toxin debate into proper perspective, since not all people feel that there is a problem. Some contend that there is an acceptable limit of toxins. This argument befuddles me. We need to stop rationalizing this nonsense and avoid this subjective argument altogether. Any rationalization of acceptable limits is merely lulling ourselves into accepting a broken system.

Toxins are bad. Period. We've been taught this since our parents showed us the skull and crossbones on the chlorine bottle when we were kids. So when (if as 4-year-olds we could understand what was toxic) did we become complacent regarding the plethora poisons that surround us?

The challenge lies in that fact that it's not always as obvious as a skull and crossbones on a bottle. That's my aim—to make the dangers more evident. I'm going to put a big virtual skull and crossbones on most things you should avoid.

We know toxins are in the environment. A U.S. EPA report in 2002 declared that we collectively released in excess of seven billion pounds of over six hundred different types of chemicals into the water and air. Seven billion pounds! How does this translate into understanding their effect on humans? Unfortunately, there is no exact method to ascertain what a non-toxic level to humans represents because we are all physiologically unique, and controlled studies are all but impossible. What we do know is that 'no toxins' is better than 'some toxins'. I know this sounds juvenile, but since we know so little about what a safe dose is, it seems irrefutable to strive for anything other than zero.

There are examples of toxins' effects everywhere. Some of the most troubling sources are items our children interact with on a daily basis, including toys, shower curtains, and vinyl flooring. The average person would never have thought that these items could be a detriment to our children's health, but studies have shown that the phthalates (a humanmade chemical) found in these everyday household items is indeed entering our children's bloodstream. What effect this has on our children and us, is highly debatable. However, some experts believe they are affecting reproductive development, and potentially acting as endocrine (i.e., hormone) disruptors[1].

The evidence is piling up. We are beginning to understand toxins' effects on the human body, in both the short and long term. What will be the next banned substance that we have been treating as benign? Asbestos, and BPA, have been past culprits.

Before we get into all the various chemicals and sources of these chemicals, let's develop an understanding of how they can affect us. When discussing toxins' effects on humans, there are two main categories for classifying adverse chemical exposures: *toxic chemical reactions* and *chemical sensitivities*. It is important for people who believe they have been exposed to a chemical to try and distinguish between the two, to correctly determine a course of action.

A toxic chemical reaction is an acute response from exposure to a particular chemical. Typically, the symptoms are similar for all exposed, and heighten in severity as the chemical exposure increases.

Someone who has a particular chemical sensitivity can become progressively more ill even as the exposure levels decrease. The symptoms are often unique, and isolated to each case, which is why diagnosing chemical sensitivities can be difficult. Acute reactions to a chemical are possible, but chronic, multiple chemical sensitivities are more likely.

Our bodies need to work overtime to deal with this modern chemical overload. Many of these toxins and heavy metals are fat-soluble, and therefore must be processed by the liver, then eliminated from the body through either the bowel or the kidneys. This process gets sabotaged by our overburdened livers, and can evolve into a chemical sensitivity. In this scenario the liver is unable to keep up with the amount of toxins it is required to process, allowing these toxins to build up in the body; particularly in our fat and bones.

The liver—though an important player in detoxification—isn't alone in the body's fight to eliminate toxins; it is supported by five other channels of elimination, namely the kidneys, bowel, lymphatic system, lungs, and skin. They all work together in an attempt to rid the body of waste. But we are chemically over-exposed as a society, and these channels often cannot keep up. As Doris Rapp highlights in *Our Toxic World: A Wake Up Call*[2], symptoms associated with chemical sensitivities often include headaches, sensitivities to smells (e.g., perfumes), numbness, and skin irritation. These symptoms can be immediate, or can manifest over days and weeks. For some, exposure can lead to severe brain and nervous system damage, resulting in memory loss, or physical and mental debilitation.

Rapp goes on to highlight that in the U.S., upwards of seventy million people are believed to have chemical sensitivities of some kind. Many of these people have reactions to the most benign of sources, such as paint or perfume. Often individuals who are chemically sensitive have pre-existing conditions such as asthma, or allergies, which can make them even more sensitive to toxins, and often worsen their condition. Of those affected, approximately ten million are so severely affected that they cannot function normally outside of a sterile environment. It is incredible how unaware we are of this pervasive issue.

Chemicals in Our Environment

Source	Effects	How to Avoid
Chemical: Triphenyltin (herbicides)		
Antifungal paints and fungicides	Permanent adverse effects on one's immune system.	Pay attention to chemical declarations and avoid those products.
Chemical: Organichlorides (pesticides)		
Still often used on lawns under the chemicals 2,4-D and 2,4,5-T, and treated wood	Linked to higher incidences of cancer, such as lymphoma.	Opt for natural fertilizers and question how your deck wood has been treated.
Chemical: Organophosphates (pesticides)		
May be sprayed in municipal parks and common areas, under the chemical malathion	Shown to cause serious nervous system damage.	Question your municipality on how they control pests. Control where your children play.
Chemical: Carbamates		
Clothing, and plastics	Not as toxic as some of the previously listed chemicals, but may affect several organs.	Ensure clothes are washed before wearing. Organic fabrics are ideal, however they are not always practical to obtain.
Chemical: Phthalates		
(In the fumes of) floor tiles, plastics, shower curtains, and various adhesives	Believed to act as serious endocrine (hormonal) disruptors.	This gets tricky. Replace what can be replaced, such as shower curtains. Opt for wooden toys if practical.
Chemical: Solvents		
Common solvents are benzene, toluene, and xylene	Adverse effects can range from cancer to kidney damage.	Ensure there is ample ventilation if you ever need to use solvents. Avoid breathing them in.

We're getting closer to understanding the issue, what's out there, and a few particular offenders. Let's now check out the wide range of symptoms you may be experiencing, due to chemical sensitivities and heavy metal toxicity. Many of us go years with symptoms, without being able to identify the root cause.

Here is a list of potential symptoms of chemical sensitivity:

- fatigue
- headaches
- attention deficit
- muscle aches
- itchy eyes, and runny nose
- coughing
- joint pain
- metallic taste
- ear, nose, or throat infections
- rashes
- insomnia
- gastrointestinal distress
- unusual behavior

This list is not exhaustive and only meant to be directional in nature. Our challenge lies in the fact that many of these symptoms are non-specific, meaning that there can be several different causes, and are often lived with and accepted. Nonetheless, some chemical sensitivities or heavy metal toxicities can be detected, and treated. A visit to a naturopathic doctor is advisable if you suffer from any of these symptoms.

It is important for a person to assess the ailments they have, and then attempt to find and remove the source. It is often not enough to eliminate the source, as many toxins are fat-soluble and need to be actively removed. Food sensitivities may behave in a similar fashion, in that you can remove the food, but detoxification and healing need to occur for your system to rebalance itself. In both cases, naturopathic medicine has holistic techniques to help detoxify and rebalance the body.

I Just Ate What?!

If you were aware of the chemicals used to grow your conventional food, you might think twice before chowing down. In fact, the EPA reported that in 2007 approximately 857 million pounds of conventional pesticides were used in the U.S. alone, with about 80% used on cropland. This amount represents nearly three pounds per citizen! Is this truly necessary for us to grow our food? Even with all these chemicals being used, yield loss due to pests continues to challenge farmers. The over-application of pesticides is complicating matters further by giving birth to new superpests, which are becoming stronger and more resilient.

Perhaps coincidentally—though I find it highly doubtful—our children are increasingly being diagnosed with autism, allergies, attention deficit, and cancer. These correlations are becoming increasingly difficult to accept when we are finding babies that are being born with measurable levels of various chemicals in their blood, such as DDT, DDE, and PCBs. Babies are literally being born toxic. And these chemicals are not shown to be inert either; as correlations have been made between weight gain and exposure to these chemicals—potentially due to these chemicals acting as endocrine (i.e., hormone) disruptors[3].

Toxic exposure starts at childbirth, with chemicals deposited and stored in our fat tissue over the years. A 1996 EPA report found that adults over the age of forty-five had over five times the levels of chemical pesticides in their fat stores, compared to children under the age of 14[4].

And things are not improving. As I've harped on repeatedly, today we're exposed to massive amounts of pesticides and herbicides, in and on our food, with chemicals once deemed to be safe, such as BPA (often a component in old baby bottles), now outlawed in certain countries. What other apparently safe chemicals on the market today will be deemed dangerous in the future?

Our food contains several chemicals of which we need to be aware. The Environmental Working Group—a leading American environmental health research and advocacy organization—has done an excellent job outlining the most contaminated conventionally grown foods and those with the least pesticide contamination, as outlined in the following table:

The "Dirty Dozen" and the "Clean Fifteen"

"The Dirty Dozen"	"The Clean Fifteen"
Apples	Asparagus
Sweet Bell Peppers	Avocados
Pears	Cabbage
Celery	Cantaloupe (Domestic)
Tomatoes	Sweet Corn
Grapes	Eggplant
Cherries	Grapefruit
Nectarines	Kiwi
Peaches	Mangos
Potatoes	Honeydew Melon
Spinach	Onions
Strawberries	Pineapples
	Sweet Peas (frozen)
	Cauliflower
	Watermelon

Fluoride

I'd like to now focus on one chemical that we regularly ingest, under the guise of 'safe for consumption'—fluoride. Many of us still use fluoridated toothpaste, drink fluoridated water, and grew up with fluoride treatments. Remember when the dentist used to soak your teeth in fluoride for 10 minutes or so? It was sold to the public on the premise that it strengthened our enamel, yet added fluoride is not essential for human health, dental or otherwise.

Fluoride, like many other fat-soluble toxins, accumulates in our tissues. Although much of the fluoride you ingest exits your body, the vast majority of what remains is absorbed and accumulates in tissues such as teeth, bones, and blood vessels. Certain nutrients bind to fluoride, working to reduce its accumulative effects. However, no amount of fluoride is acceptable.

Besides being commonly known as a carcinogen, fluoride is associated with compromising your immune system, brain damage, and accelerated aging. Educate yourself on what is in your water, and choose fluoride-free toothpaste. Why take unnecessary risks when you don't need to?

> ### *Ikkuma* INFO: MERCURY
>
> Up to 50% of dentists in the U.S. still use dental amalgam for fillings, which hovers at around 50% mercury content. Mercury is a well-known vaporous neurotoxin that builds up in fatty tissue, especially the brain. It can seriously harm your kidneys and create a host of neurological issues. It is still used by dentists because it's quick and easy. Amalgams are also one of the biggest sources of mercury in the environment, where even minute amounts can contaminate water tables. Don't expose your children to this threat.

What You Don't Eat Can Still Hurt You

We're exposed to countless toxins that we do not ingest, at least not knowingly. Unbeknownst to many out there, toxins creep into our bloodstream via our biggest organ, the skin. Take the nicotine patch as an example. It's applied on the skin. The medication is absorbed through your skin into your bloodstream. The technical term for this is transdermal absorption. That's why knowing what goes on your skin is so critical, yet so often underestimated.

We repeatedly try to convince ourselves that spending the extra money for organic, or even simple natural products, isn't worth it. You know that feeling when you save $3 on your sunscreen and are ecstatic that your saving a few bucks. In the end, what's $3 when, for the next two months, that crap will smother your body, and your child's body, every time you get sun exposure.

Not everything that touches your skin gets absorbed, but a heck of a lot does. When you go cheap on what goes in or on your body, the only person your cheating is yourself. You know this. And trust me, there are measurable consequences.

Toxins that you apply topically can be contained in anything from make-up to soaps to skin lotions. I also lump electromagnetic fields from cell phones in this category. We cannot possibly address all the dangers that exist, but the following table lists some of the most common sources, and what you can do to protect yourself:

Common Sources of Chemicals in Your Daily Life

Average Number of Chemicals	Most Dangerous	Associated Issues	How to Avoid
Product: Shampoo			
>10	Sodium lauryl sulphate, tetra sodium, propylene glycol	Irritation, possible eye damage	Read the label and look for organic, or find natural sources without these chemicals.
Product: Eye Shadow			
>25	Polyethylene terephthalate	Organ damage, links to cancer, hormonal disruption	There are many natural, or organic options for make-up and cosmetics. Read the label.
Product: Lipstick			
>30	Polymenthyl methacrylate	Allergies, links to cancer	There are many natural, or organic options for make-up and cosmetics. Read the label.
Product: Fake Tanner			
>20	Various parabens	Irritation, hormonal disruption	Get some sun instead.
Product: Perfume			
>200	Benzaldehyde	Links to kidney damage, irritation of the mouth and throat	Essential oils are chemical-free. Many excellent perfumes offer these options.
Product: Hairspray			
>10	Octinoxate, isophthalates	Hormonal disruption, allergies, irritation of the throat and eyes	Read the label. These toxins become airborne, and you breathe them in.
Product: Foundation			
>20	Polymenthyl methacrylate	Allergies, links to cancer	There are many natural, or organic options for make-up and cosmetics. Read the label.
Product: Body Lotion			
>30	Various parabens	Irritation, hormonal disruption	There are hundreds of organic options out there.

i. Sunscreens

I want to bring special attention to sunscreens—the product that we have been sold on as safe, and obligatory for any sun exposure. This campaign to justify sunscreen's mandatory use is probably one of the most lucrative fear campaigns ever conducted. And this one involved vilifying the sun.

Since sunscreens are so ubiquitous, I think it's worth highlighting some of their dangers. Writer D.H. Lawrence aptly sums up our relationship with the sun, "If we think about it, we find that our life consists in a relation with all things; stone, earth, trees, flowers, water, insects, fishes, birds, creatures, sun, rainbow, children, women, other men. But his greatest and final relation is with the sun." Sadly, over time, we have grown to fear the sun. I wholeheartedly disagree with the demonization of this ball of energy that gives us life. My greatest fear is not the sun, but the lotions we put on our bodies to seemingly protect us. Sunscreens may be one of the most egregious topically-applied toxins we subject our bodies to on a regular basis.

The Environmental Working Group's *2012 Sunscreen Guide* requires the following to make it on its 'safe list':

- contains no oxybenzone or retinyl palmitate (form of vitamin A)
- maximum spf of 50 (anything stronger is throwing money away)
- full spectrum protection, i.e. UVA and UVB

Astonishingly, as reported in the sunscreen guide, only 25% of tested sunscreens are considered free of harmful chemicals and effective at protecting your skin. Remember, many chemicals you put on your skin can find their way into your bloodstream.

Ironically, many sunscreens may be increasing our risk of skin cancer, and possibly promote the spread of cancer due to their harmful ingredients, namely oxybenzone, retinyl palmitate, and various parabens. Let's take a look at these main offenders and claims against them.

Due to its ability to absorb UV rays, we find oxybenzone in approximately half of the sunscreens sold. Some believe it is linked to hormonal disruption and cell damage, potentially leading to cancer. Despite these claims, the FDA still considers it safe and approved for everybody over the age of six months.

CNN brought light to the dangers of our second offender—retinyl palmitate—in a feature, reporting that, "Government funded studies have found that this particular type of vitamin A may increase the risk of skin cancer when used on sun-exposed skin." Significant amounts of this chemical are readily absorbed through the skin, amplifying the risk[5].

Let's wrap up the discussion by looking at one of the most common ingredients to which we are exposed, not only in sunscreens but also in all lotions—parabens. Parabens are chemicals with estrogen-like properties, often referred to as xenoestrogens. Take note that over time excessive exposure of seemingly-innocuous estrogen has been linked to increased risk of breast cancer. The EPA has linked methyl parabens to hormonal and neurological disruption as well as various cancers. Yet, we still find parabens in many common skin lotions.

Besides reading ingredient labels and making better choices (i.e., organic), when looking for effective sunscreens, you should always ensure that they are broad spectrum. Doing this will help protect you against both UVB (responsible for sunburns), and UVA rays (can lead to skin damage, and aging). Regarding SPF, you should target between 15 and 50 SPF.

> *Ikkuma* **INFO: UVA VS. UVB RAYS**
>
> UVA rays have a longer wavelength than UVB rays, allowing them to pass through the atmosphere much more effectively. Later in the day our atmosphere actually reflects most UVB rays, while letting UVA rays pass—similar to winter months in the northern hemisphere at any time of day. The bad news is that the rays we want to get are the vitamin D inducing UVBs. UVA rays are most associated with skin damage and cancer. So, get your sun in the middle of the day in moderation and make sure you don't burn.

Your children may be at risk of long-term ailments due to the products they are exposed to, such as sunscreen; and all this happens under the claim that these products provide the necessary protection. Bottom line, if you are buying sunscreen, look for organic alternatives that use zinc or titanium oxide as the active ingredient to protect your skin. There are many great products out there. As mentioned, the Environmental Working Group has a great sunscreen guide, where sunscreens are ranked in terms of safety.

When getting sun exposure, it is always a good idea to err on the side of caution. I often suggest starting out with 15 minutes of sun, and, as tolerance increases, try to extend this length of time. Remember that the sun is a good thing. Amongst many other benefits, controlled exposure to the sun is a very rich source of vitamin D, whose benefits includes, but are not limited to, the following:

- protects against cancer
- key ingredient for a healthy heart
- helps maintain ideal blood pressure
- supports your immune system

The sun is not our enemy. It is necessary for all living things and, when respected, is key to long lasting health.

ii. Household Products

We have a slew of chemicals in our homes at any given time. If you take a look at the ingredients in your laundry detergent or air fresheners, you will get a taste of the dozens of chemicals you're potentially exposed to on a daily basis—it isn't feasible to list them all. But again, since the effects aren't immediately felt, we think we can get away with cheap, synthetic products. We can do better.

We have access to more natural and organic choices than ever before. It could be as simple as finding a more environmentally-friendly laundry detergent, or using essential oils to freshen up your house, instead of chemical air fresheners. Essential oils (found in most health shops) are void of synthetic chemicals, making them better choices for freshening up your house or apartment.

As I touched on earlier, even our clothes can contain toxins. One example, nonylphenol ethoxylate (NPE), is found in many fabrics and detergents sold in the U.S., yet it's banned in Canada, Europe, and several other countries. When introduced in the environment, NPE breaks down into a chemical called nonylphenol. Once it makes its way into the water, it can build up in fish, and wildlife. NPEs are a type of xenoestrogen. When NPEs are ingested, the organism responds to it similar to how it responds to estrogen. This is highly toxic, and affects the development of the organism. Beyond these hormone-disrupting properties, chemicals like NPE may have many other wide-ranging side effects[6]. Admittedly this is difficult to manage, but we should be pushing our governments to be more vigilant and grant us more sustainable options.

iii. Cell Phones

Cell phones represent one of the most disruptive technologies in human history. Now with the advent of smart phones, their impact on our daily lives continues to reach far beyond what we could have imagined even ten years ago. Although cell phones have ostensibly improved our quality of life, the jury is still out on the potential damage that they can have on our health.

Although you may not yet be convinced that cell phones are potentially dangerous, I'm sure many of you have heard reports that the radiation they emit, and electromagnetic fields (EMF) they create, are causes for concern. These potential dangers have caught the attention of the World Health Organization (WHO), who issued a report claiming that cell phones may be carcinogenic (i.e., rated as a Class B Carcinogen), due to their radio frequency electromagnetic fields[7].

In reality, the actual power of a cell phone is quite weak, but even when you are not on a call, it emits very erratic radiation, which can potentially interfere with DNA function. We do know that our organs are sensitive to radiation and electromagnetic fields. Unfortunately, since cell phones are still relatively new, we don't yet know the long-term effects of prolonged cell phone use on humans. There are, however, several studies out there that link cell phone use to increased cancer rates and tumors, in particular for women and children[8].

Other studies have shown that EMF radiation compromises cell membranes, allowing heavy metals to build up in our system. Heavy metals—such as mercury—have been shown to negatively impact neurological function, especially in children.

Similar to the discussion regarding GMOs, why not err on the side of caution? I'm not saying ditch the cell phone, but there are ways you can lower your risk:

- avoid carrying your cell phone near your body (i.e., within six inches is most dangerous), or put it in airplane mode
- use a headset for phone calls
- heavily restrict your children from talking extensively on cell phones (I know that this is nearly impossible)
- use a landline when possible (if you have access to one)

Now that I've inundated you with all the toxin-talk you can handle, I'd like to leave you with a few last comments. I apologize for exhausting the argument to be wary of toxin exposure in our lives. However, it is important to become aware of the disturbing health trends that seem to coincide with our dependency on chemicals. For instance, in 2012, (according to the CDC) 1 in 68 children in the U.S. were diagnosed with autism spectrum disorder (ASD), rising from 1 in 150 children in 2000. Many believe that this rise stems from the increased daily toxic exposure to which kids are now subjected. Others have cited the increase in recommended vaccines as the big culprit. Either way, it is a disturbing trend that needs to be better understood.

When it comes to our health and the health of our children, there shouldn't be an acceptable level of risk. We must do what we can to minimize toxin exposure. Eating organic, eliminating toxins from the home, reducing electromagnetic fields (e.g., cell phones, especially in the bedroom), and scrutinizing what you put on your skin will minimize the risk.

Time to Detox

On a daily basis, the average American will need to detoxify their bodies of hundreds of chemicals. Our overtaxed liver is the super organ that takes the brunt of the pain when dealing with all these adulterants. Let's briefly look at how the body deals with toxins.

The first phase of detoxification is hepatic (i.e., detoxification occurring in the liver). In this phase, a number of nutrients are needed to support the liver's ability to detoxify. Through a series of reactions in the liver—aided by nutrients such as B vitamins—toxins get converted into a form suitable for excretion. Once the liver performs its magic, these toxins either travel to the gall bladder where bile taxis it to our colon for elimination, or the kidneys excrete the toxins via the bladder. If these pathways get clogged, the toxins are either stored inside the body, or eliminated through the skin.

To deal with this daily barrage of chemicals, we need to ensure that we consume large amounts of healthy foods to obtain the nutrients required for detoxification. A healthy diet will help keep the pathways for detoxification running efficiently. Moreover, avoiding late night meals will allow the liver to finish processing food shortly after midnight, giving it time to recuperate for the busy day ahead.

The body stores toxins—that do not get eliminated—in fat and tissue. In cases of excessive fat loss, these toxins can rush back into the bloodstream. This process requires even more B vitamins and amino acids to deal with the toxic overload. Although this is technically possible, once a toxin penetrates fat and tissue it is tough to detoxify naturally. It is important that this is treated on an individualized basis since we all have varying levels of toxic stress.

Depending on the types of toxins and levels in the body, severe health consequences may result, such as various cancers and neurological disorders. It would be advisable to seek out a naturopathic doctor for rigorous detoxification.

To assess your toxin or heavy metal levels, you can ask a certified health professional to perform a chemical screen of your blood and urine. If you have elevated levels of toxins or heavy metals in your system, seek professional help to detoxify. Naturopathic medicine offers a trusted, individualized approach to removing toxins from the system.

If you are going to try a gentle detox, and depending on the severity of your toxic levels, a great reference for do-it-yourself detoxifying is the book *Natural Detoxification: A Practical Encyclopedia: The Complete Guide to Clearing Your Body of Toxins,* written by Jacqueline Krohn and Frances Taylor[9].

> *Ikkuma* **INFO: DAILY MORNING CLEANSE**
>
> Here is what I consider a great morning routine for mild detoxification of the liver. Before eating breakfast, immediately take ½ ounce of fresh lemon juice and drink it with 16 ounces of water. The benefits are unbelievable for something so simple, as it:
>
> - Helps flush our organs, especially the liver, and kick-starts our metabolism
> - Improves our alkaline/acid profile, that is, it promotes alkalinity
> - Helps to purge toxins from the body first thing in the morning, which is great for everything, including our skin
> - Stimulates the birth of new blood and muscle cells
> - Helps cleanse the colon, allowing for better nutrient absorption
> - Supports our lymphatic system, helping to fight infection
>
> Following this initial glass of water with lemon juice, drink another glass of water, then wait approximately 30 minutes before eating a healthy breakfast. This will give your body enough time to prepare itself for some real food.

The Marvels of Modern Medicine?

> *"Always laugh when you can. It is cheap medicine."*
> —Lord Byron, English romantic poet

I've attempted to keep my arguments balanced throughout the book, while ultimately subscribing to a more holistic approach to health (i.e., looking at health from all angles). I believe that a holistic approach leads to a more sustainable and healthy way to live. Despite my beliefs, the conventional health industry reigns supreme (as a percentage of dollars spent), with pharmaceuticals being the foundation of this industry.

When I say conventional health 'industry' we need to understand what this implies. We're dealing with an industry, not unlike the automotive industry. As such, this industry tracks metrics as any other business would. Do you think that a pharma CEO is more concerned with how many patients' lives their drugs improved, or how their profits are trending in the present quarter? I can't speak for every CEO, but I would bet that the next board meeting will focus on profit projections.

I have come from industry, so I'm not blaming capitalism per se. What I'm attempting to do, is help you realize that even in the health industry, we are dealing with corporations. These corporations have a duty to their shareholders to make as much money as possible. In doing so, there may be times when CEOs base decisions on the benefits to shareholders, regardless of how it affects the average main street citizen. Only you can be responsible for your health. Not your doctor, and surely not a pharmaceutical company.

i. Pharmaceuticals

Pharmaceutical drugs are typically designed to treat a person's symptoms, rather than correct the root cause of the problem. But even understanding what symptoms a drug is meant to alleviate is tricky at times. Judging by your average commercial, who the hell would know what any drug is supposed to do? These commercials would have you believe that every time you take a drug, regardless of the symptoms, you get teleported to some picturesque field, where the flowers are in bloom, and children are frolicking in the lilies. This panacea that the drug promises does not exist. For many, reliance on pharmaceuticals represents pain and suffering.

Drugs can also be very expensive, and involve a seemingly unending rainbow of potentially adverse reactions. Just pay attention to the speed talker at the end of every drug commercial.

To influence legislation on their drugs, big pharma spends tens of millions of dollars lobbying federal governments. In the U.S., lobbyists outnumber congressman by approximately two to one (this obviously changes year over year). This 'lobbying' has many outcomes, from suppressing alternative medicine, to gaining favorable rulings on potential legislation.

One such example of legislation occurred in the 1990's, when direct to consumer drug advertising was allowed. Since then, the number of chronic drug users has ballooned. The Associated Press reported that as of 2007, 25% of U.S. children took medication on a regular basis for 'chronic' conditions.

Drugs are now touted as necessary for prevention of chronic illness. Drugs you used to take occasionally, are now encouraged to be taken daily. Common chronic medications include ADHD pills, anti-depressants, statins, and hormone replacement medications.

Aspirin is a classic example of an overused drug. Many doctors claim that it lowers the risk of recurrence for cardiovascular events in patients. Thus, many doctors recommend taking it daily.

There are now several findings showing that aspirin does not improve a patient's chance of living longer. In fact, some argue that, because it thins the blood, aspirin conceals greater issues until it is too late—the result being a major cardiac event, instead of a gradual onset of symptoms. Moreover, the side effects of aspirin are well documented, warning mainly of damage to the intestinal tract. Instead of taking aspirin, maintain a healthy heart by following the guidelines throughout this book.

Exacerbating this already dire situation, the FDA is becoming less capable, and potentially lacks the will to deal with the power of big pharma. As Dr. David Graham, the famous whistleblower of the Merck pharmaceutical's Vioxx scandal (i.e., a recall of all Vioxx due to reports of cardiovascular events associated with the drug), stated in 2005, "As currently configured, the FDA is not able to adequately protect the American public. It is more interested in protecting the interests of industry. It views industry as its client, and the client is someone whose interests you represent."[10]

Again, I'm not demonizing all Western medicine. I'm just suggesting adequate due diligence, before counting on pharmaceutical companies to act in your best interests. It's incumbent upon you to understand how the drugs you are taking work, and their related side effects.

Instead of alleviating the symptoms of our various ailments with drugs, we should be focused on understanding the respective root cause. The reliance on pharmaceuticals to mask our unhealthy lifestyles has reached pandemic proportions. We're becoming a chronically medicated generation that depends on drugs for survival. We need to alter the way we leverage modern medicine if we wish to survive as a species. We should relegate Western medicine to crisis management. Functional and holistic medicine offer much safer solutions for chronic ailments. But proactivity is the ultimate solution. Nurture your body with the proper sustenance it needs to thrive—not pharmaceutical drugs—to live with vitality.

ii. Vaccines

I've had many heated disagreements with friends regarding vaccines. I'm convinced that we would be in a much worse position if we didn't have vaccines. Yet, I'm not convinced that our children require the barrage of vaccines now prescribed by the conventional health industry.

Since the advent of the smallpox vaccine in 1796, scientists have developed hundreds of vaccines. The general understanding of how vaccines work is as follows: your body's immune system recognizes the vaccine as a foreign invader. With the help of adjuvants (i.e., chemicals added to the vaccine to prompt an immune response), your body then creates the necessary antibodies, and destroys the invader. If you become exposed to this invader in the future, your body would recognize the invader, and already be equipped with the antibodies to prompt an immune response. Albeit oversimplified, this paints a rough picture.

Despite the necessity of certain vaccines, have we now taken the use of vaccines too far? For example, do we need flu vaccines? My generation didn't rely on flu vaccines. We fought the flu bug, and our immune system was bolstered commensurately. Think of it as the body gaining wisdom. Making matters worse, by the time you get the vaccine for a distinct flu strain, it's often too late for it to be effective.

Society is becoming so dependent on vaccines that we may be creating a generation with compromised, weakened, and unseasoned immune systems. I might sound alarmist, but getting a vaccine just because it's available is not the answer.

An area of controversy regarding vaccines is the growing speculation that certain vaccines have been causing cases of autism—though the majority of the scientific community refutes this claim. There was a case, however, where the Italian Health Ministry concluded that the MMR (measles mumps rubella) vaccine was the cause of a child's autism[11], but this isolated case was found to be without merit and quickly discredited.

My advice would be to administer only what is absolutely necessary (which I know is not always obvious). Just because a new vaccine is available (e.g., flu vaccines), doesn't mean you should take it. Instead, focus on nurturing your gut flora, to strengthen your immune system.

iii. Mammograms and CT Scans

Along with the evolution in medications, we have seen similar advances in forms of treatment, such as CT scans, and mammograms. These routinely prescribed treatments are, in some cases, doing more harm than good. Fear-driven abuse of medical technology is often used to increase profits.

Focusing first on mammograms, recent research has shown that regular mammograms increase the risk of breast cancer. I'm not at all suggesting that women avoid mammograms, but they should understand that this routine exam is not without its dangers. Women should question their practitioner regarding the frequency, and necessity, of mammograms.

Most of us are not aware that a mammogram can expose a woman's breast to nearly 1000 times the radiation of a chest x-ray. Unbelievably, according to Dr. Epstein and Dr. Bertell, if pre-menopausal women follow a typical mammogram screening protocol, they would be exposed to 5 rads of radiation. This is comparable to the radiation people experienced within one mile of Hiroshima and Nagasaki[12]. Knowing this, is it surprising that there have been many studies showing clear correlations between regular mammograms and breast cancer?

There are alternative breast cancer detection methods available. Ask your doctor about Digital Infrared Imaging. This method of testing can detect changes in breast tissue behavior, and does not contain any radiation.

Another common diagnostic tool that involves significant radiation is the CT scan. Although they can be instrumental in diagnosing head injuries, and cancer, CT scans have associated dangers. Recent research concluded that kids have 3x the risk of developing brain cancer after just a few CT scans[13]. And as capitalism would dictate, the amount of CT scans is skyrocketing. As reported by CNN Health[14] in 2008, CT Scans have seen a "five-fold increase in 14 years".

If you're prescribed a CT scan:

- ask if an ultrasound or MRI could be a potential substitute
- ensure that it's necessary
- request the lowest level of radiation possible

Individualized Medicine

"What is food to one, is to others bitter poison."
—LUCRETIUS, ROMAN POET

If I've dissuaded you from adopting a future plagued with pills, you may be asking yourself, "Okay, not what?" To achieve and maintain the highest level of health and wellness, diet, supplements, and treatment should be individualized.

Everyone is unique. Genetically, physiologically, biochemically, and constitutionally. Whether for health maintenance, or disease treatment, it is imperative that you assess your individual needs.

Naturopathic medicine applies this philosophy in its practice, using time-honoured forms of assessment, such as Traditional Chinese Medicine (TCM), and homeopathy. Although I will not be digging into it in detail, Ayurvedic medicine is another age-old method that incorporates different techniques to ensure the body is in a state of balance.

In TCM the individual's constitution is paramount in choosing the treatment for illness, and understanding imbalances. Tongue and pulse diagnoses are used to assess the health and function of the organs, fluids, and blood of the patient. Based on the findings, the appropriate treatment is chosen, which typically includes a combination of herbs, acupuncture, and a tailored diet. TCM views food as medicine, where conventional Western medicine often takes one-size-fits-all approach for assessment and treatment, and relies too heavily on prescription medication.

Let's use blood pressure to illustrate these differences in philosophy. In North America, conventional treatment would involve following a particular drug protocol to reduce blood pressure. If one drug doesn't get your blood pressure to the desired level, they try another, and so on. Assessment and treatment are most commonly based on a standard protocol, and not on the specific needs of the individual.

With TCM, five people may all come in at a similar stage of high blood pressure, but, based on their constitution and diagnosis, they would likely be treated differently. Rather than focus on the patient's symptoms, treatment would aim at balancing the individual, and addressing the unique origin of the condition.

The second of the more holistic forms of healthcare is homeopathy. Homeopathy is one of the most widely used forms of medical treatment around the globe. It is inexpensive, safe, and efficient. A massive study conducted in 2011 by the Swiss government on complementary forms of medicine—which included homeopathy—added much credibility to the practice.

Homeopathy operates according to the philosophy that "Like Cures Like." It matches the individual's constitution or illness 'picture' with a homeopathic substance that will create a similar picture in a healthy person. This practice is believed to address the imbalance that leads to the disease on its highest level, hence isolating the cure.

Food Is Medicine

Now that we have established that food is medicine, let's analyze an individualized program that will help you design your optimal eating regimen, namely metabolic typing. Remember that when we look at personal diets and programs for health maintenance, as well as for illness treatment, we must consider several factors for the program to have optimal benefit. These could include, your current state of health, nutritional deficiencies, risk factors for disease, family history, personal health history, food sensitivities, genetics, and constitution.

Let's do a deep-dive into metabolic typing to demonstrate how we can create a bespoke diet. Introduced by orthodontist William Donald Kelley, metabolic typing involves catering your nutritional needs to your unique metabolism. Merriam-Webster defines metabolism as 'the chemical changes in living cells by which energy is provided for vital processes and activities, and new material is assimilated.' Kelley leveraged his understanding of diverse types of metabolism to develop the Kelley Cancer Therapy, which proposed that proper foods for an individual could help combat the deadly disease.

As seen in other forms of individualized nutritional protocols, metabolic typing surmises that we all have a different make up or constitution. As such, we respond differently to nutritional inputs. In effect:

- we are as unique on the inside as we are on the outside
- this inherited uniqueness affects physiological systems, structures, and metabolism of cells, implying that we may have individualized nutritional needs

You can liken this to the several different makes of cars. While they all look different on the outside, what we don't see are the vast mechanical differences on the inside. Some run better using regular unleaded gas, while others run better with premium-unleaded gasoline. Think of metabolic typing the same way. Some people run better on a high carb regimen, some on a high (meat) protein regimen, and some need a mix.

We have age-old techniques of assessing our imbalances, and a variety of methods to develop individualized nutritional plans. Why haven't we learned from all this readily available knowledge? Unfortunately, gratuitous corporate and pharmaceutical profiteering has created a society dependent on medication to maintain a symptom-free life; which is very different from a healthy life. If you need to be kept alive by statins (i.e., cholesterol lowering medication), or pills to maintain normal blood pressure, then there is something fundamentally wrong.

Allopathic (i.e., conventional) medicine is predicated on this premise; that we should be treating the symptoms of a condition, not the underlying cause. There is much more money to be made in keeping someone alive on drugs than curing the underlying biochemical imbalances, which make up the roots of chronic disease. We need to be the counterpoint to this big pharma reality. We need to make the decision to (proactively) create the health we want.

Remember, a holistic approach to health deals with the root of the illness by correcting the hormonal, nervous, and energy production systems, so that biochemical imbalances (i.e., disease) cannot thrive.

This approach to health helps ensure that you:

- effectively treat the root of, and prevent, chronic illnesses
- sustain health by dealing with your imbalances
- treat any condition holistically; treat the body, not the symptom
- allow your body to perform what it was designed to do—heal itself

It's time to stop the cycle. Avoid toxins as much as humanly possible. Toxins in every form—including pharmaceutical drugs—are potentially life threatening. Wean yourself off chronic medication by arming your body with the nutrients it needs. And stop categorizing organic and natural options as discretionary expenses. They're not. Stop bemoaning the cost of quality foods, and make sacrifices in areas of your life that aren't crucial to your vitality.

Ikkuma Top *Toxins... The Ugly Truth* Tweets:

- **Be aware of common toxins**, such as solvents, paints, and lawn fertilizers.
- If you choose to eat conventional foods, **be aware of the biggest pesticide offenders** in the produce aisle. http://bit.ly/10srL15
- **Lose the fluoride toothpaste.** Fluoride is a known carcinogen. Many cities are banning it from their drinking water.
- In North America, **mercury is still often used in dental fillings**. Mercury can seriously harm your kidneys and brain. Choose safer options.
- Our skin is our biggest organ. Protect it! **Several skincare products, like soaps and lotions, contain known toxins.**

- Many sunscreens contain harmful oxybenzone, and parabens. Opt for organic alternatives. http://bit.ly/ZT9lY5
- **Sun in moderation—without sunscreen**—is healthy. Shorter wavelength UVB (vitamin D producing) rays are at their peak at midday.
- The World Health Organization deems the **electromagnetic fields associated with cell phones as possibly carcinogenic.** Use a bluetooth device.
- **Choose natural laundry detergents and fabric softeners.** Most household products have several chemicals that we may breathe in and absorb.
- **The liver is exposed to hundreds of chemicals daily.** Eat nutrient-rich foods to support detoxification. Try lemon juice in water for a morning flush.
- **Vaccines have been a medical marvel,** however, they can cause adverse effects. Scrutinize which ones you choose. Do you need a flu shot?
- **CT scans deliver high levels of radiation.** Although necessary for severe head trauma, they should be a last resort. http://bit.ly/11wQk47
- **Mammography has been linked to increased incidences of breast cancer.** Opt for alternative screening methods, or reduce mammogram frequency.

Bonus Ikkuma *Toxins... The Ugly Truth* Tweets:

- **Don't put plastic in the microwave.** Placing plastics in the microwave potentially accelerates its leaching into food and beverages.
- **Avoid xenoestrogens.** These chemicals are notorious for disrupting your hormones. Find them in plastic bottles, pesticides, and PVC curtains.

- **Use essential oil**—liquids containing volatile aroma compounds—based perfumes. They are a safe and effective way to smell good.
- **Know your anti-bacterial soap.** Many of these soaps contain triclosan, which has been linked to endocrine disruption. http://bit.ly/10EtLc5

Section
FOUR

Keeping the Body 'Tuned Up'

(Ikkuma Translation: Stoking The Fire)

"Look not mournfully into the past. It comes not back again. Wisely improve the present. It is thine. Go forth to meet the shadowy future, without fear."
—HENRY WADSWORTH LONGFELLOW, 19TH CENTURY AMERICAN POET

The foundation of lasting health involves proper nutrition, exercise, the elimination of toxins, a good nights sleep, stress management, and a positive attitude. Having touched on the critical role your external environment plays in maintaining your overall health, let's now look inwards and investigate how the environment that we create in the body can either bolster our constitution or work against us. The role our internal environment plays in genetic expression (i.e., the turning 'on' and 'off' of your genes) is a relatively recent topic of study that further sheds light on our ability to control our fate. We need to take control of our physical well-being before our body takes control of us.

Now that we've postulated that it is indeed you that (predominantly) controls your fate, what are your health goals? What do you want to achieve? Once you understand your goals, you must be honest with yourself, and ascertain the limits of your resolve. Ask what you're prepared to do, set your priorities, and begin making a plan. And to be frank, your motivation—be it vanity or holistic health—are inconsequential, in that it will be your level (not your source) of motivation that will ultimately predict your chances of success.

Don't find yourself in the excuse trap that enables inaction. Health and self-care don't belong in the discretionary category. There will always be excuses, such as not having time because of the kids, or your job. Creating healthy routines will make these excuses less and less justifiable.

You may not immediately feel the effects of neglect, but you will down the road. You know this. Health and wellbeing is a life-long journey. Start implementing changes that you will be able to sustain. Take it one step at a time. If you are just starting out, be realistic. The key is to consistently move forward.

In this final section, as we explore stress, sleep, and fitness, I will attempt to define the importance of each concept, followed by ways to improve. It is a slight change of gears, in that we are now addressing how we treat our bodies versus how we nourish our bodies. Although this section will take more effort on your part, if you want to take control, this next section is critical. It will change your life forever.

Stress... The Silent Killer

> *"He who is of calm and happy nature will hardly feel the pressure of age, but to him who is of an opposite disposition, youth and age are equally a burden."*
> —Plato, Greek Philosopher

Stress gets a lot of press these days, and rightfully so. There is a constant barrage of warnings that chronic stress will eventually lead to disease. Despite this, the average person does not understand or acknowledge how stress manifests itself inside their body.

For many of us, since we will only feel the deleterious effects of stress, five, ten, or fifteen years down the road, we tend to ignore it. We rationalize our destructive lifestyles, convinced that we don't need to change, that it's not a problem.

It's critical that we educate ourselves, and start understanding how our behavior affects our bodies. Will it take a heart attack to for you to believe that stress kills? For many it does. Have you had a heart attack? Have you spoken to someone who has had a heart attack? Have you seen the aftermath of open-heart surgery? It's a little worse than taking five minutes (on a regular basis) to be present and calm. And that job you pine over, if it's killing you, then it might be time to take a look around at the things you love and assess your priorities. Again, this isn't my call, nor is it a judgment. But if things need to change, it is you that will need to lead that change.

i. Physiological Response

> *"It is the mind that makes the body."*
> — SOJOURNER TRUTH, 19TH CENTURY AMERICAN ORATOR

There are many different sources of stress and responses to stress. Unfortunately, discussing the specific physiological response of stress is never black and white. There are infinite degrees of stress, thus infinite responses by your body. The sources and nature of stress have evolved over time, much like human society has, but our body's physiological response has remained relatively consistent.

For our ancestors, stress may have come from being chased by a bear. Their body's natural defenses would kick in, prompting that well-known rush of adrenaline, along with a rush of cortisol (i.e., the 'fight or flight' hormone). This stress would prompt their bodies to switch from daily life—repair and digestion—to survival. Their heart rate would skyrocket, blood sugar would spike, and senses would heighten.

This response to a perceived threat (i.e., stress), helped keep our ancestors alive. However, it is meant to be followed up by the 'rest and digest' (i.e., parasympathetic) phase.

Today a bear is not likely chasing you, but maybe you can't pay the bills, or pressure at work doesn't let up. Though you may not have life-threatening stressors, modern day chronic stress prevents many people from transitioning back into the parasympathetic phase, forcing their bodies to exist in the sympathetic condition of fight or flight.

A chronic sympathetic state leads to adrenal exhaustion, lowered immunity, high blood pressure, insulin resistance, and excessive cortisol. Although necessary for survival, in excess, cortisol breaks down muscle (i.e., catabolism), increases blood pressure, and releases glucose and fatty acids from the liver. It also blunts insulin sensitivity, and adds to that dangerous visceral fat around your abdomen.

The gut is one of the primary victims in this chronic state of stress. Gut health and stress are inextricably linked. Our gut has the second highest concentration of neurons, with our brains having the lion's share. The gut, therefore, is essentially our second brain. Those butterflies in your stomach, or that 'gut feeling', are all examples of how your gut, and emotions interact with each other.

Chronic stress has a detrimental effect on our gut health through:

- severely decreasing enzyme production—enzymes are catalysts for metabolic reactions (e.g., digestion)
- reducing absorption of essential vitamins and minerals
- compromising gut flora population
- delivering up to four times less blood flow to your digestive tract

"Meditation—Sit in the stillness of your center and let your grounded energy radiate peace."—S. LeBlanc

ii. Stress Management

"Laughter is the most healthful exertion."
— CHRISTOPH WILHELM HUFELAND, 18TH CENTURY GERMAN PHYSICIAN AND WRITER

"Never continue in a job you don't enjoy. If you're happy in what you're doing, you'll like yourself, you'll have inner peace. And if you have that, along with physical health, you will have had more success than you could possibly have imagined."
—JOHNNY CARSON, AMERICAN COMEDIAN

It is not a secret that diet and exercise are vital for maintaining optimal health. Diet is the foundation for all health. So, it's no surprise that stress is directly affected by diet. The angle I will take regarding stress and diet's interdependency is not what you may think. Yes, substances like caffeine may induce anxiety and stress due to the predictable adrenaline rush, but the biggest concern lays in the physiological stress certain foods place on the body.

Refined carbohydrates, such as white bread, sugar, high-fructose corn syrup, and processed foods high in salt, all have a hand in putting your body under undue stress through promoting chronic inflammation. Explained earlier, chronic inflammation is an immune response brought on by the body to address and heal the damage from a poor diet. Eliminate the culprits and reduce inflammation.

Besides diet, exercise is a foundational activity that will help you manage stress. Apart from potentially distracting you from your sources of anxiety, exercise prompts positive, stress-reducing physiological responses within the body. Exercise produces several 'feel-good' hormones, such as norepinephrine, serotonin, and dopamine, which can help tame your feelings of stress and anxiety. Listening to music while exercising is also a great idea, as it can help both improve your workout, and your mood, respectively.

As a fun interlude aimed at immediately reducing your present stress levels, I'd like to give you a quick exercise and a few tips on how you calm the mind. It's a simple 5-minute breathing-with-intention exercise. We take oxygen for granted but it can be immensely therapeutic. While this exercise only takes a few minutes, it can immediately lower your blood pressure and heart rate:

- breathe in through your nose for a 4-6 count
- hold for a 1 count
- exhale through your mouth for a 6-8 count
- during the entire exercise focus on all your body systems involved in breathing (i.e., nostrils, diaphragm, stomach, and lungs)
- repeat this 10-15 times

Here are several other ways to maintain a more peaceful lifestyle:

- be present and aware
- be compassionate and kind to others—favor respect, dignity, and tolerance
- add sweetness to life—decrease what feels sour or bitter
- indulge in nature—spend time in nature and appreciate its beauty
- be calm within yourself—don't add to the agitation that surrounds us
- be of service—not only to friends and family, but others in need
- breathe deeply (i.e., from the diaphragm)—avoid shallow chest breathing
- meditate daily—I suggest a minimum of 15 minutes every morning
- be grateful—keep a gratitude journal and update it daily

I can't stress enough (I know... bad joke) how important it is to manage this silent killer. Remember that if you don't find sure-fire ways to combat the stress in your life, and reframe it in a positive light, then you could be at risk for several adverse health issues.

Ikkuma Top *Stress Management* Tweets:

- Eating healthy foods is crucial if you wish to eliminate physiological stress in the body. **Processed foods are inflammatory, adding to stress.**
- Take a break for **5 minutes to just breathe**. Breathe in through your nose, hold, and out through your mouth. This will quickly reduce hypertension.
- **Meditation,** once associated with shamans and yogis, is now mainstream. And its incredible benefits are being noticed http://huff.to/13cqNHG
- **Laughter** can have stress-busting and blood-pressure-reducing effects. Try to get at least five hearty laughs daily.

- **Smiling** isn't just a sign that someone is happy. The act of smiling can help with recovery after stressful events. http://bit.ly/10CKHuO
- **Outdoor exercise** has been shown to directly improve well-being, with the greatest effect in areas around water. http://bbc.in/ZTnvbU

Sleep...The Body's Time to Heal

"Cycles—Circadian rhythms work
to keep our bodies in sync with
our inner workings and our outer
environment."—S. LeBlanc

"Take a rest; a field that has rested gives a bountiful crop."
— OVID, ANCIENT ROMAN POET

There's someone in every crowd who claims that they don't need more than a few hours of sleep. So what they're telling us is that after millions of years of evolution, they are the genetic anomaly that doesn't need sleep. (True, between 1-3% of the population have a genetic ability to survive with little sleep, but this is exceptional.) Maybe these people represent a disruptive evolutionary shift that will be the new normal. Chances are, they're not. Most everyone needs ample sleep. In this section, I'll illustrate you how you can give yourself the best odds for a restful sleep.

What is sleep? This question may seem idiotic. Yet, there's significant information regarding sleep of which many are still unaware. I'll add a little context, by digging into the anatomy of our critical sleep cycle, or circadian cycle.

In the morning, our blood pressure and temperature increase to stage our bodies for the upcoming day. By mid-morning we become fully alert, and our metabolism ramps up. All the while, sunlight is helping keep us awake and alert (during the day) by suppressing our melatonin (i.e., our sleep hormone).

Our metabolism typically peaks sometime around mid-afternoon, when we're at our physical and mental best (after that post-lunch nap?). Once the evening arrives, our metabolism starts to calm, and our body's temperature starts to drop—all in step with increased production of melatonin. Melatonin, often referred to as the sleep hormone, is critical for regulating sleep patterns. When we fall asleep, melatonin has peaked, and our body is in a state of repair and rejuvenation. This sleep cycle is referred to as our circadian rhythm.

Without boring you with too much science, I will briefly dig a little deeper into the circadian rhythm's significance. Everybody has an internal clock called the Suprachaismatic Nucleus (SCN), hardwired to the eyes. Think of this as the orchestra conductor. When the sun sets, (in the absence of artificial light) this 'conductor' prompts our pineal gland to produce melatonin. This process is necessary to keep the body synchronized, prompting our cells to work in-step.

When we mess with this process, through inconsistent sleeping patterns and sabotaged sleep, our body is no longer in tune. Instead of Beethoven, our body has become a bad contestant from American Idol.

Very few of us get enough sleep, while even fewer seem to understand the consequences of inadequate sleep. It is my hope that, after learning more about sleep, and the significant effect it has on our overall health, more of you will start to make it a priority.

i. Why Is Sleep Necessary?

How many times have you heard, "I don't need more than four hours sleep"? Or maybe, "I would love to get more sleep, but I just can't find the time." I have questioned countless people about how much sleep they think they need. Astoundingly, many people see it as a badge of honor to not get much sleep.

Many seem to think they are the exception to the rule that humans need sleep. I challenge these individuals not to set their alarms, eliminate all noise from their rooms, and track how long they sleep. I guarantee it will be more than 4-5 hours. Your body knows what it needs, so give it the opportunity to get the rest it requires to keep everything functioning as it should.

We typically hear that between 7–9 hours of sleep per night is sufficient. Research has shown that sleeping less that six hours increases insulin resistance, thus increasing the risk of diabetes. Other recent studies have shown that less than five hours of sleep increases your risk of developing heart disease and having a stroke. The American Cancer Society published the results of a study they performed on one million adults. It showed that an inadequate amount of sleep significantly increased the risk of several cancers, potentially linked to sleep's effect on our immune system.

Proper sleep has also been linked to reduced rates of breast cancer. In fact, some studies argue that inadequate sleep, not diet, is the primary cause of breast cancer in women. That is, melatonin (which is stimulated by darkness) slows down the production of estrogen, which in excess has been shown to promote breast cancer. Predictably, there is a strong correlation between breast cancer incidence and artificial light in the evening. It is amazing that the simple invention of the light bulb has had such a monumental impact on human sleep cycles. Edison's creation has been short-changing our sleep cycles with little or no resistance.

David Suzuki highlights, in the documentary *Lights Out*, the detrimental effects of artificial light at night. One relevant example is the relationship between shift-work—which disrupts our circadian rhythm—and cancer. The *Nurses Health Study* followed over 200,000 nurses and found that those with at least twenty years of experience increased their cancer risk by 79%. Moreover, the World Health Organization (WHO) has now lumped shift-work in the same carcinogen-risk category as UV rays, and diesel exhaust. Other studies estimate that shift-workers have double the risk of getting cardiovascular disease. Even if you aren't a shift-worker, this clearly shows what can happen when sleep is compromised.

> ### *Ikkuma* **INFO: MELATONIN FRIENDLY LIGHTS**
> Research has shown that the visible light's blue spectrum is responsible for melatonin suppression. This knowledge has motivated companies to start designing lights that mimic the soft white glow from lights we're used to, without the melatonin-suppressing blue wavelengths. This has also made it to our smartphones and computers, with apps that filter these wavelengths. This will do wonders to help improve melatonin levels right before bed.

The Golden Rule of sleep is quite logical: you want to give your body the sleep it needs to be able to sustain energy—without stimulation—throughout the day, and allow for ample time to rebuild and rejuvenate at night. When this necessary sleep is compromised, it can wreak havoc on the body. Here are a few examples of the detrimental effects lack of sleep can have on your health:

- significantly compromises your immune system
- can cause migraines
- impairs memory function
- promotes tumor growth, in that melatonin suppresses cancer cell growth
- increases your risk of cardiovascular disease

Sleep is your body's time to repair. It gives your organs a needed break. The average person underestimates the serious consequences of ineffective sleep patterns. It is virtually impossible to be healthy in the long run if you do not manage your sleep habits. Regardless of how much you work out, or how well you eat, if you don't sleep you are going to encounter serious health issues down the road.

ii. How Do You Optimize Your Sleep?

Let's break down the key ingredients for a 'good' night's sleep, and focus on a few things to avoid to reduce the chances for a 'bad' night's sleep. A restful sleep is predicated on two main factors: following a rhythm (i.e., circadian rhythm), and eliminating all noise—mental, environmental, and physical.

As explained, in an average day, you should wake up feeling rested, and later in the day become gradually more tired. As the sun goes down, producing less and less light, your body will increase melatonin production, ideally reaching peak fatigue right before bed. If you expose yourself to artificial light in the evening, it will reduce your melatonin levels right before bed. Artificial light can suppress melatonin production for up to 90 minutes, even after the lights are shut off.

Messing with this (circadian) rhythm is extremely common, as a lot of people have erratic sleep patterns, particularly during the weekend. I'm guilty of this as well. We don't live in a bubble, so I'm aware that there are challenges in getting consistent sleep. You can catch up on sleep during the weekend, to some degree, but even this (seemingly innocent) sleep change can mess with your brain's rhythm. So, try to maintain a fairly routine sleep schedule to keep your circadian rhythm in tune. To ensure your body is ready to hit the hay as planned, skip the long, extended naps throughout the day, and refrain from drinking caffeinated beverages later in the day.

The second major factor for a sound sleep is eliminating all noise. Mental noise could be in the form of stress and anxiety; physical noise could be something as simple as a chronic pain; and environmental noise can include things like the lights on your alarm clock, or having your blinds open. Even the minimal light from your alarm clock can suppress melatonin when you are sleeping. Your room should be completely free of any light. For children who like the lights on at night, choose red night-lights, in that they emit a light that doesn't suppress melatonin.

It's important to focus on why we aren't sleeping, and tackle the root of the issue, rather than just addressing the symptom: insomnia. With that said, many people unfortunately turn to ineffective pharmaceutical drugs to treat their insomnia. According to the FDA, many over-the-counter sleep aids have little effect on improving sleep.

Even more shocking, a National Health Institute study of prescription sleeping pills showed their extremely marginal benefits (on average only minutes of improvement per night) versus a placebo. We're trying to medicate our way to sleep, which is not only unhealthy, it's futile.

Getting a good night's sleep is not as complicated as people make it out to be. Check out these *Ikkuma Top Sleep... The Body's Time to Heal Tweets* for a summary of how you can leverage sleep to give your body what needs to be at optimum health.

Ikkuma Top *Sleep... The Body's Time to Heal* Tweets:

- **Try to maintain your circadian rhythm.** Regularly changing your sleep patterns confuses your body. The orchestra gets out of synch.
- **Avoid bright lights at night,** as they suppress melatonin production for up to 90 minutes after they've been shut off. Dim the lights and avoid TV.
- **Black-out your bedroom.** Small amounts of light can disrupt your production of melatonin and serotonin, affecting sleep and mood.
- **Eliminate noise.** If you live in a noisy neighborhood, wear earplugs. Even mental chatter is noise, so try to maintain a calm and peaceful mind.
- **Avoid late night caffeine**, as it can disrupt your sleep. Be aware that even midday caffeine can have adverse effects. http://bit.ly/10lkggp
- **Skip long daytime naps.** Long naps can short-change your circadian rhythm. Stick to 15–25 minute naps to get a needed boost.
- **Deal with chronic stress.** It affects every part of your health including sleep. Anxiety can promote adrenaline and cortisol production.
- **Steer clear of artificial sleep aids.** The sleep aid market is booming despite showing marginal improvements. http://bit.ly/YQXtuH

Bonus Ikkuma *Sleep... The Body's Time to Heal* Tweets:

- **Reduce electromagnetic fields in your bedroom.** EMFs can disrupt the functioning of your pineal gland, thus affecting melatonin.
- For late night bathroom breaks, keep the lights off or **get a red night-light**, since blue light can quickly suppress melatonin.
- **Cool down your bedroom.** Your body temperature drops when you sleep. Turning down the temperature in your bedroom will mimic this change.

- **Lose the alarm clock** or try to find one that gradually wakes you up. Abruptly waking up can spike adrenaline and cortisol.
- **Get a memory foam mattress.** They transfer much less energy when you are restless in bed. This helps with a restless partner.

Fitness... Use It or Lose It

"Opening—Reach past where you have been before and watch how the world opens up to meet you."
—S. LeBlanc

"A man too busy to take care of his health is like a mechanic too busy to take care of his tools."
— SPANISH PROVERB

Let me guess... you don't have time to exercise? Don't even get me started on this one. I bet if someone slapped you in the face every five minutes, until you found forty-five minutes, three days per week, you would find the time pretty darn quick. It's all about motivation, driven by necessity. If it's a deemed a necessity you'll do it. Fitness should be deemed a necessity. Assess your priorities, lost the excuses, and start to move.

Exercise is crucial for a long, healthy, and vibrant life. Exercise will keep you mobile well into your later years, helping you feel younger, while living longer. Besides the obvious benefits of maintaining a healthy body weight, exercise reduces the risk of diseases like cancer, diabetes, osteoporosis, and cardiovascular disease. It also helps to reduce depression through promoting dopamine and serotonin production, while bolstering your energy, and improving cognitive function[1].

With that brief but impressive resume how can you not make time for exercise?

Before we start, you need to understand and galvanize your specific goals, or underlying motivation, for getting fit. Maybe you want a beach body, or maybe that spare tire is what drives you? Regardless of your motivation, the tips and guidelines in this section will help guide you on your fitness journey.

Everyone is different. Each of us has different physiology, genetics, and lifestyles. Based on your internal make-up, you can modulate your intensity and routine to achieve the desired results. It's not unlike your diet, in that there are different avenues for specific goals. No matter what healthy eating habits you choose, you will be promoting an environment in your body where disease cannot thrive. The same goes for fitness. By incorporating adequate amounts of aerobic and resistance training into your regimen, you'll develop a body that looks great, helps your physical performance, keeps you energized, and helps you fight disease.

Ikkuma INFO: KIDS AND FITNESS

It is widely believed that children should not engage in resistance training of any kind. This is a fallacy. We already know that it is very important for children to exercise. One of the ways they can get this exercise is through resistance training. Obviously, supervision and a reasonable workout program are important, but there is no reason why kids cannot benefit from a resistance training regimen from a qualified trainer.

I'm not talking about throwing them in a weight room to lift heavy weights. I'm talking about a more benign approach, such as using their own body weight, and employing equipment such as resistance bands (i.e., elastic bands designed for exercise) or stability balls. It is more important than ever to encourage kids and adolescents to step up to the plate and get active. As is the case for adults, kids can reap benefits ranging from increasing bone density and maintaining healthy body-fat percentages, to improving cognitive function, reducing their chance of injury, and improving performance in sports. The world has changed. Childrens' diets have become riddled with fat-inducing high-fructose corn syrup, and outdoor activities have been replaced with game consoles and computers; causing the rate of childhood obesity to skyrocket. So, get kids active... their bodies will thank you for it!

General Muscle Types

Your muscles are composed of two primary muscle fiber groups: slow-twitch, and fast-twitch. Slow-twitch (type I) muscle fibers are typically employed under relatively light activity. They have a high level of endurance but generate little force, compared to their fast-twitch siblings. As such, it takes very different training protocols to elicit growth within each group. People who focus on endurance sports, such as rowers and marathon runners, would typically rely more on their type I fibers.

The second major group of muscle fibers, your fast-twitch (type II) muscle fibers, are recruited when you do explosive movements, or are lifting heavy loads. Fast twitch muscles are further distinguished as type IIa and type IIb. Type IIa, which can take on the characteristics of both fast and slow twitch fibers, have relatively more endurance, versus type IIb fibers, which can generate more force. The more you stimulate fast-twitch fibers, the faster and fuller your muscles will grow. Slow-twitch muscles do not have the same scale of growth. This distinction isn't only necessary for a 'beach body'. It's of paramount importance if you want to build a fat-burning factory. The more lean muscle you build, the more calories you burn.

Fast-twitch muscles also contain fibers that are efficient at storing glycogen. Although this is dependent on your diet, as these fibers grow fuller it will allow for increased glucose absorption. This growth will help contribute to maintaining healthy insulin sensitivity and blood-sugar levels. When engaged, these growth-stimulating fibers also prompt the body to produce human growth hormone, which has been shown to have anti-aging effects.

The key to efficiently activating both your slow and fast-twitch muscles is to work out at high intensities (e.g., speed, load, instability, and tension), with a good combination of aerobic and resistance training. Initially, your slow twitch muscles (i.e., more endurance and recover rapidly) are recruited through aerobic activity, followed by the fast twitch muscles (i.e., the power center—promote growth), via dynamic resistance training, or any activity that requires quick and responsive movements (i.e., plyometrics, such as jumping).

Aerobics vs. Resistance Training

I've been working out for over twenty years. While I have seen minor fluctuations in my weight, and fat percentage, I have maintained a lean body composition. I do this without performing (virtually) any regular aerobic activity.

Don't get me wrong; I have nothing against aerobic activity. Obviously doing anything more strenuous than sitting on a couch will burn incremental calories, and help you lose fat. However, building lean muscle mass through resistance training is crucial, as the more lean muscle mass you have, the more calories you will burn—at rest—throughout the day (i.e., basal metabolic rate). In fact, approximately 70–85% of your calories burned will be during the time you aren't training[2]. It's estimated that due to an increased basal (i.e., base) metabolic rate, every added pound of muscle you put on burns between 5–10 incremental calories per day. So, adding just 5–10 pounds of muscle will help you burn between 25-100 extra calories per day, without you having to do anything different. The calorie burning doesn't end there. A strenuous, high-intensity workout, ramps up your metabolism for 36–48 hours following the workout, while your body is busy repairing and transforming your body to deal with its new demands.

If you want to thrive, if you want to maintain healthy bones and tissue, if you want to have that vibrant body that looks great, you should strongly consider incorporating some form of high-intensity training into your regimen. Let's now dig a little deeper into how to effectively introduce both aerobic and resistance training into your lifestyle.

Aerobic Training

On a purely aesthetic level, simply doing moderate cardiovascular exercise will not build a powerful body. Aerobic exercise primarily recruits your slow-twitch fibers. As we have learned, fast-twitch muscle fibers ignite the greatest overall muscle growth. So, if a better physique, improving heart health, and reducing body fat, is the end goal—regardless of your gender—the right type of high-intensity aerobic training is crucial.

When it comes to exercise, we are all starting from different places, so it's important to be aware of your limits. Walking may be a great place to begin for those who have just decided to take this journey, though it should not end there; as it won't coax the body to prompt significant change. It is a beginning, not necessarily the solution.

Yet, too much of anything, including cardio, can be harmful to the body. While its adverse effects are entirely dependent on the individual, long bouts of cardio (well in excess of an hour) can:

- cause the body to produce excess cortisol that, as explained earlier, is catabolic (i.e., breaks down tissue—such as muscles—for energy), and may lead to several chronic issues
- weaken your immune system
- damage the heart for up to three months when taken to the extreme, such as running marathons without sufficient training[3]

With that said, the consensus is that any intense training surpassing an hour, be it aerobic or resistance training, can promote excess production of cortisol—switching the body from an anabolic state (i.e., constructive metabolism) to a catabolic state (i.e., destructive metabolism)—and compromise your immune system.

Aerobic Training Guidelines and Benefits

One effective way to get the most out of your cardio workouts is to employ interval training. Interval training is a 'sprint and rest,' or 'sprint and light-work' method of cardio training that is both aerobic (i.e., prolonged, moderate exercise) and anaerobic (i.e., short duration, high intensity). Much like the wisdom of our hunter-gatherer ancestors' diet, we can also learn a lot about how they pushed their bodies. They had bouts of intense activity with rest periods, which is what this workout is designed to mimic.

While there are many variations to these high-intensity intervals, they typically employ a pattern of sprinting for a short period at high intensity, then resting (rest method), or lowering the intensity (light-work method) for a period, and repeating as desired. The particular protocol is entirely dependent on the individual. The key to this style of workout is the ratio of work to rest, or work to light-work. For a beginner, aiming for a 1:4 ratio would make sense. Meaning that for every second of intense activity, you are resting, or reducing the intensity, for four seconds. For instance, you would follow-up a thirty-second sprint with a two-minute rest period. Make sure you have a proper warm-up and cool down.

There is no magic formula because there are many variations of high-intensity intervals. As long as you aim for 10–20-minute routines, you should be hitting the sweet spot of effectiveness.

Remember, the body is composed of slow-twitch and fast-twitch muscle types. Unless you employ explosive movements, extend muscle time under tension, add significant load, or incorporate high-intensity interval training into your cardio, you will be relying (predominantly) on the slow-twitch muscle fibers. This high-intensity-interval is designed to challenge the body, and employ all muscle-fiber types.

Here is a high-intensity interval that I swear by for efficient and effective cardio:

- Begin with a proper warm-up before getting into the intervals. There are many different ways to achieve this. Proper dynamic stretching, with potential foam rolling, and ten minutes of light cardio would be a good start. When choosing cardio equipment, note that low impact cardio machines can include an elliptical trainer or stationary bike, while moderate impact cardio can involve a treadmill or running outside (depending on the surface). If you have a beach go for it! You'll not only reduce the impact on your joints, but you'll incorporate 'earthing' (see *Ikkuma Info: Earthing*) as an added health benefit
- After warming up, increase the intensity of the exercise to what you can maintain for only 20–30 seconds, and go hard. Once you finish the sprint phase, rest for twice as long as you sprinted, representing a 1:2 protocol (i.e., if you sprinted for thirty seconds, you would rest for sixty seconds). I repeat this cycle 8–10 times in succession, but for a beginner you may choose to start with a 1:4 protocol, with fewer cycles in succession, working your way up over time. It is important to progress according to your fitness level

- Once you have finished the intervals, initiate a proper cool down. This could include approximately three minutes (depends on fitness level) of low-intensity cardio or walking, followed by some static stretching or self myo-fascia (SMF) release, such as foam rolling (see *Ikkuma Info: Foam Rollers*)

Ikkuma INFO: EARTHING

Earthing involves walking barefoot on the earth. As Dr. Oschman explains in *Energy Medicine: The Scientific Basis*, when you walk barefoot, free electrons from the earth are conducted into your body. These free electrons act as antioxidants. Since we are often wearing shoes, we fail to reap these benefits on a consistent basis.

We already know that antioxidants are essential agents in maintaining healthy free-radical levels in the body. Free-radicals are brought on by many factors, including chronic inflammation, and poor eating habits. Though often vilified, they also factor in the healing process. When bacteria have penetrated your skin, or you have damaged cells, free-radicals will help break them down. But if free-radicals get out of hand and leak into healthy surrounding tissue — an occurrence typically caused by chronic inflammation — you open yourself up to DNA damage. Earthing can be an effective way to combat this inflammation. The ideal location for earthing is the beach, as seawater is an excellent conductor. However, walking barefoot anywhere in nature will do the trick.

Ikkuma INFO: FOAM ROLLERS

Foam rolling a muscle is a fantastic way to maintain healthy soft tissue and muscle health. It essentially irons out kinks in soft tissue, like muscle fiber. When you train a muscle hard, you tear myofibrils (i.e., individual muscle strands), resulting in muscle growth when they heal. Over time, training can lead to adhesions and scar tissue in your muscles and soft tissue. Even if you don't train, and are stationary for long periods of time, you can create tightness your muscles that can be aided by foam rolling.

There are many foam rolling techniques. Simplified, you place the roller on the floor and rest the muscle or soft tissue directly on the roller. Apply as much pressure as you can handle, then roll the area back and forth about six inches in each direction. Foam rolling lengthens the muscle, helping break down the adhesions or knots, in turn allowing for better blood flow, and quicker recovery. The best time to do this would be following a workout. A few minutes of rolling makes a world of difference. You can get foam rollers at most fitness stores. They look like oversized hollowed out rolls of paper towel with about an inch of foam over the entire outside surface.

Here are some benefits from performing intervals:

- you effectively work both your aerobic, and anaerobic, energy systems
- after the age of thirty, our human growth hormone and testosterone levels begin to decline, accelerating the aging process. Intervals have been shown to naturally increase the production of human growth hormone (HGH) by over 500%[4]
- studies show that high-intensity intervals improve cardiovascular endurance more than a purely aerobic cardio session, in a much shorter time[5]
- it can take up to forty-eight hours for fast-twitch muscles to fully repair, translating into increased metabolism and fat burning during these two days

Resistance Training

What jumps to mind when I say resistance training? Visions of muscle-bound meatheads? I'm hoping, due to increased education on its many benefits, that this is becoming less and less the case.

Resistance training—better known as weight, or strength, training—is performing exercises against a force to increase the size and strength of your muscles. Several studies have shown that, compared to aerobic training, it is a more efficient way to shed fat.

Muscles need energy to function. As touched on earlier, the more lean muscle you develop, the higher your basal metabolic rate, which in turn burns more calories at rest. This energy needs to come from somewhere. It can originate from the food we eat, or from the energy stores in our body—the primary sources being glycogen and fat. The more energy we expend, the more fat we will eventually burn off.

Here's some basic knowledge that will arm you with the information you need to start your new workout regimen today:

i. Resistance Training Guidelines

Let's review a few terms before we get into the guts of the discussion:

- **Repetitions, Sets, Exercises:** there are "x" number of repetitions in a set, and "x" number of sets of an exercise. So, when you see 4 sets of 12 repetitions for a particular exercise, such as bench press, it implies that you are performing 48 bench presses in total. There are endless combinations of sets, repetitions, and exercises available to provide the results you desire

- **Volume:** I will mention this a few times. Volume refers to the total amount of weight lifted during a workout

All muscles have both fast-twitch and slow-twitch fibers in varying proportions. It is important to understand the underlying physiology of these different muscles. As an example, muscles like your quadriceps (i.e., your large leg muscles as seen from the front) are predominantly composed of fast-twitch fibers, whereas your smaller calf muscles are composed mainly of slow-twitch fibers.

Just remember that explosive movements, heavy weight, tension, instability, and volume stimulate the most growth. It is important to be aware, though, that different muscles do respond better to certain lifting protocols. I would encourage you to research the different major muscle groups, or elicit the help of a personal trainer to learn more. For our purposes, I will keep things at a general level.

> ### *Ikkuma* **INFO: MACHINE VS. FREE WEIGHTS**
> When you load a muscle—using bands, free weights, or machines—it will respond. Your fitness goals will dictate how you choose to load your muscles. If you just want to look good, then it doesn't make a significant difference which method you choose. You can get bigger muscles by using any apparatus that will load them sufficiently (70–85% of the maximum weight you can lift one time for that exercise is a good estimate), promoting growth.
>
> But, if your goal is overall functional strength, then free weights and compound movements (i.e., movements involving many different joints, such as the squat) are most effective. Compound movements, while typically working your largest muscles, may also recruit muscles that help maintain stability for daily activities (i.e., stabilizer muscles). I design all my workouts with compound movements using free weights. Other ways to recruit your stabilizer muscles, include static or dynamic moves on unstable surfaces.

ii. Anatomy of a Workout

It's important to give you a breakdown of all the different aspects of a workout, from stretching to post-workout. Yet, I'm not here to give you a personalized workout, as that would be impossible to do (effectively) without knowing each individual. I simply want to enable you to create some basic and efficient workouts that will serve you going forward. And, understanding that everyone is busy, I want this overview to provide you the greatest physical bang for your workout buck.

Stretching and warming-up

Stretching is a crucial part of a balanced fitness program. The flexibility that stretching provides is vital for injury prevention. While you can possibly avoid the adverse effects of poor flexibility in the short term, it will limit your fitness potential and increase your chance of injury.

There are two main types of stretching, namely static and dynamic:

- Static stretching: involves holding a body movement for an extended period, perhaps 10–30 seconds. It could be as simple as stretching your hamstring by extending your leg on a chair, and holding it in place, with a neutral spine (i.e., straight back)

- Dynamic stretching: involves movements, where the muscle is put under tension for short periods. One simple dynamic stretch is to swing each leg like a pendulum. Start with small swings and make your way up as high as you can comfortably kick for about 20–30 swings per leg

There is a time and place for both static and dynamic stretching. On non-training days, and after workouts, I would suggest static stretching. Static stretching before a workout can increase the risk of injury by temporarily weakening the muscle, and decreasing performance[6].

Before workouts, I would incorporate a quick round of dynamic stretches, and a pre-lift routine. Pre-lifting can involve performing lighter weight, functional moves. For instance, if I was preparing for an upper-body workout, I would perform a quick set of push-ups, pull-ups, and potentially some dips. I would then execute a single shortened, and lightweight, set of each exercise (preceding the particular exercise) planned for the workout.

This routine activates (i.e., wakes up) your nervous system, warms up your muscles, and prepares your body for the task at hand. There are many other techniques one can use to warm-up before a training session, such as foam rolling and walking. Doing a proper warm-up cannot be underestimated, as it is key for exciting the nervous system. A primed nervous system will be that much more effective when called upon to stimulate the muscle systems employed during your workout.

Workout Design

If I incorporate cardio into my workout, I place it at the end, and I remember to keep the total workout to under an hour. After a resistance training session, your glycogen reserves have been significantly depleted, potentially priming you to burn more fat during the cardio phase; though this is dependent on the intensity of your workout, and your diet. When you decide to perform your cardio—either before or after your weight training—will ultimately depend on your personal goals. People who are less inclined to do cardio may benefit from cardio before a workout.

Before we move on to the next section, I want to explain a few things. There are an infinite amount of great programs that can be drawn up for resistance training. My focus, therefore, will not be to provide you with training programs but to equip you with fundamental knowledge on how to best train your muscles for strength or growth, how to stage sets, and to provide you with some highly effective exercise protocols.

One term I would like to explain—as it pertains to lifting—is eccentric (i.e., the lengthening phase of a muscle). It is important to understand the benefits of the eccentric movement in an exercise. It is essentially the lengthening, or negative phase of a lift (i.e., when the weight is approaching the ground). For example, if you were doing a bench press or squat, this would refer to the lowering phase. Many studies show that this part of the movement prompts the best metabolic response in a muscle. Typically, try to focus on a 2:4 tempo, meaning you take 2 seconds on the concentric (i.e., shortening phase) phase and take 3–4 seconds on the eccentric (i.e., lengthening phase) phase to optimize your lifts. You can use this as a general rule for most training goals.

Growth and Strength

Muscle growth and strength are correlated; however, there are techniques that will help you to focus on one or the other. It is not only the size of your muscle, or strength, which factors into what you can lift; your nervous system also plays a significant role in your lifting ability. So if your goal is to lift heavy weights, you need to train your body to do so. I know, this seems obvious, but there is a wealth of science behind how people can increase their strength. In the next few paragraphs, I'll attempt to give you a very simplified overview of different training protocols to achieve different results.

If you're training for *muscle growth*, aim for 8–12 repetitions per set, and perform 3–4 sets per exercise. Try to allow for 90 seconds of rest between sets of the same muscle group. With this type of training protocol, you want to push your muscle to a point where you could potentially squeeze out one more rep at the end of each set (just before failure), to prompt an optimal metabolic response. When you fatigue your muscles, your body responds by repairing and growing the muscle.

If *strength* is your focus, then performing 3–5 repetitions—at approximately 90% of your maximum lift—per set, has been shown to be most efficient. Again, when I speak of percentages of your maximum lift, it means the percentage of what you could lift one time. For our purposes, in this case, you would choose a weight that you can lift 3–5 times. You are conditioning your body to lift this heavier weight. Typically you should perform about 3–5 sets of a given exercise, and give yourself longer breaks to ensure you properly rest the muscle between sets. Your energy systems usually require about 3-4 minutes to recover from this type of strain.

Logic would then suggest that a mix of these two protocols would be a comfortable split to achieve growth and strength gains. This advice is a simplification, however, and does not take into account the make-up of each muscle.

Women often approach me desiring neither significant growth, nor significant strength improvements. They are looking for moderate increases in growth and strength, but more importantly, they're looking for improved muscle tone. To improve muscle tone and endurance, employing higher repetition sets—in the range of 15–20 per set, for 2–4 sets per exercise—should achieve the desired effect.

Remember our discussion on the different fibers in a muscle—type I, type IIa, and type IIb. When you want to grow a muscle you need to activate your type II fibers, especially your type IIb fibers. The best way to do this is by lifting relatively heavy weights, increasing tension or instability, and favoring explosive movements, such as plyometrics.

Ikkuma INFO: ISOMETRIC EXERCISES

Isometric exercises involve holding a movement for an extended period of time. For instance, holding a plank for sixty seconds would be considered an isometric exercise. Belgian researchers have found that performing these exercises tends to have the greatest effect on reducing blood pressure[7].

There are countless ways to develop a training program. The key is to mix it up. Hit your muscles a variety of ways. When forced to deal with new demands they will adjust. Logical, right?

Incorporating the advice involving strength, growth, and a combination of the two will produce healthy muscle tone and explosive vitality—as long as you learn proper technique. I recommend asking someone qualified, or enlisting a trainer for a kick-start. A little investment could do wonders for your progress.

Some women shy away from resistance training. They falsely believe that strength training will make them too bulky. The truth is that women's physiology makes it much more difficult for them to add significant 'bulk'—although bulk is admittedly a subjective term—if they follow a balanced training protocol.

As explained earlier, an increase in lean muscle mass will burn more fat. And muscle is marginally more dense than fat, so when you lose a pound of fat and trade it for a pound of muscle, you lose overall size, and become more toned in the process.

Supersets

I've been training for decades and swear by supersets. Again, this is dependent on fitness level, and experience. Supersets typically involve performing an exercise for a muscle (i.e., the agonist muscle), and then, with little or no rest, hitting the antagonist muscle. Agonist (prime mover)-antagonist (opposing) muscle groups are located on opposite sides of a bone or joint, such as the bicep (i.e., front of the arm) and the tricep (i.e., back of the arm). A example of a superset involving these two muscles would be to perform a bicep curl, followed by a tricep extension. After you complete a set of curls, you would take a very quick breather, or no rest at all, and execute the tricep extensions.

One of the significant benefits of incorporating supersets into a workout is that you perform a lot of resistance training in a relatively short period. That is, you're essentially working one muscle group while the other rests, and vice versa. There is no excuse as to why you can't have a great workout in less than forty-five minutes. Supersets also get your heart-rate humming, giving you some cardiovascular work during your training session.

> ### *Ikkuma* INFO: PRE-EXHAUSTION SUPERSETS
>
> Some supersets can also be designed to hit similar muscle groups. Below is a more complicated superset training protocol that I enjoy, which I feel incorporates the right mix of strength, and hypertrophy (i.e., growth). This may be difficult to follow for a beginner. It involves performing three different exercises for a similar muscle group. Each exercise is performed in series with little to no break, and the number of reps increases with each set. It is also known as a pre-exhaustion superset. You progress from a compound movement, to a more focused exercise, with all sets involving the same muscle group. For example:
>
> - Incline bench press (dumbbells)—6 reps (2 seconds up, 4 down)
> - Flat bench press (dumbbells)—12 reps (2 seconds up, 3 down)
> - Flat bench flys (dumbbells)—25 reps (control up-control down)

Compound Functional Exercises

I am a true believer of efficiency. I'm an engineer, so how can I not. Like I said earlier, our busy schedules have put enormous pressures on our free time, so if you can get more work done in less time then why wouldn't you? Compound functional exercises—functional moves involving multiple joints—is another surefire way, besides supersets, to be more efficient with your time at the gym, while achieving excellent results.

Compound functional exercises recruit multiple muscle groups, and are a catalyst for obtaining fantastic gains. They prompt multiple muscles to fire at once, setting the stage for an anabolic (i.e., muscle building) response in several muscles. Some excellent compound exercises are the: deadlift (activates nearly every large muscle in the body), squats (blasts your midsection, and work wonders for your lower body), pull-up (an effective judge of your fitness progress—works arms, back, and midsection), dip (great for chest, arms, and midsection), and squat-to-a shoulder press (good split between upper and lower body).

I would encourage you to look up the proper methods for all compound functional exercises, to learn how to perform them correctly. These exercises will shock your body, eliciting a significant metabolic response.

Post-Workout

It's important to fuel your muscles after strenuous workouts. During a training session, you break down muscle fibers (i.e., myofibrils), and burn hundreds of calories. What you put into your body following a workout is critical, as it will aid in muscle repair and growth, and reload your energy reserves.

A post-workout smoothie with high-quality whey protein—or a non-dairy based protein powder, such as rice or pea protein—and some form of carbohydrate, such as frozen berries, with a liquid base, is a fantastic injection of post-workout nutrients. While the exact amount of post-workout protein is impossible to ascertain, common wisdom suggests that approximately 20-25 grams of protein is sufficient for the average man, while women typically require approximately 10–15 grams. Again there is no steadfast rule, but getting healthy protein and carbs into your body post-workout is key for rebuilding and repairing muscles. Check out the *Ikkuma 'SuperHuman' Smoothie* in the *Foods To 'Live' By* section for a fantastic way to energize hard-worked muscles.

Even if you nourish your body post-workout, you will probably get some muscle soreness for a couple of days. Regardless of where it originates, the faster you can deal with it, the quicker your body will grow. I'm talking about soreness, not injury. Some falsely believe it is a build-up of lactic acid that causes the soreness, but a more accepted theory is that it's brought on by inflammation related to the micro-tears in your muscle fibers. When these tears repair, the muscle grows. Seek out products designed to help relieve, and reduce, the duration of muscle soreness to speed up recovery, such as arnica and Epsom salts (in the bath), or roll your muscles using a foam roller.

iii. Benefits

Although the most obvious benefits of resistance training are to add lean muscle mass and attack your excess fat, bone density is also positively affected. Bones are repeatedly loaded during a workout. The strengthening of bones and tendons is a physiological response to this load, helping to stave off osteoporosis. Promoting the growth of lean muscle also awakens your metabolism; accelerating it for up to 48 hours post-workout. This process increases your basal metabolic rate, helping to burn even more calories at rest.

I can't say enough about resistance training. If you haven't moved a weight in your life, please start. I promise that it will change your life almost immediately. After three months of effective resistance training, you will notice incredible changes in your body. Many of you may have been jogging for years, yet haven't seen the results you want. Start mixing it up, and the results will come:

- you'll look healthier, and more toned
- your energy levels will increase
- bones and tendons will be stronger
- insulin levels will improve, and fat will melt from your mid-section
- you'll help slow down aging

Ikkuma Top *Fitness... Use It Or Lose It* Tweets:

- **Kids need to be more active, get them training.** Using resistance bands and body weight—instead of weights—can safely build strength.
- **Strength training,** not aerobics, is the key to sustained weight loss. Lean muscle boosts your metabolism, and burns more calories at rest.
- **Embrace interval training.** Sprinting, combined with proper rest periods, can increase your aerobic threshold, and strengthen your heart.
- **Aim for workouts of 60 minutes or less.** Beyond this, your body may start producing excess cortisol, with muscle deteriorating effects.
- **Walk barefoot.** Your feet receive free electrons from the earth, which may neutralize free-radicals, reducing inflammation.
- **Start rolling.** Foam rollers can help maintain healthy muscle by ironing out kinks, lengthening the muscle, and improving blood flow.
- **Opt for free weights,** instead of machines to gain lean muscle. Free weights recruit the stabilizing muscles that help prevent injury.

- **Seek out a personal trainer** for gaining knowledge on how to train. When armed with this knowledge, you should be motivated enough to get to the gym.
- Studies have shown that brief dynamic stretching between sets (approximately 30 seconds) increases strength. Stretch more as you age.
- **Slow speed repetitions** on the weight-lowering (i.e., eccentric) portion of the lift have been shown to prompt a greater metabolic response.
- For **maximum growth,** aim for 8–12 repetitions per set and perform 2–4 sets per exercise. You grow via load, instability, or explosiveness.
- **Increasing strength** depends on more than muscle growth. It's about conditioning your brain to lift heavy loads—aim for 3–5 'significantly-loaded' reps per set.
- Studies have shown that **isometric moves** (i.e., holding a position), or simply pausing during a repetition, may reduce blood pressure over time.
- If you feel you don't have time to train, **incorporate supersets** into your workout. This can cut training time by nearly half.
- Focusing on **compound (multi-joint) exercises** is an excellent way to build balanced strength, as they recruit several different muscle groups.
- Workouts can break down muscle fibers. Feed your body the **quality protein and energy** it needs to start rebuilding. Try an *Ikkuma 'SuperHuman' Smoothie.*

Bonus Ikkuma *Fitness Use It Or Lose It* Tweets:

- **Count down during sets.** Studies show that it's motivating to focus on how many reps are left in a set.
- Before a workout, **avoid foods with HFCS or sugar.** It potentially reduces the amount of fat you could have burned during your workout.
- For **optimal running form**, land on the middle of your foot directly

under you. Landing with your foot ahead of you is like hitting the brakes.
- **Love your dips and pull-ups,** as they develop your shoulders, chest, arms, back and core, and are an excellent measure of overall fitness.
- **Protect your back with good posture.** For all exercises keep a straight back—pump out your chest like a proud lion, keep your shoulders back, and stick out your butt.
- Incorporate a **high-volume workout** into your regimen to accelerate growth. Look up German volumetric training for an example.
- **Train at least three times per week.** I'm sure that brushing your teeth isn't discretionary; fitness shouldn't be either.
- **Bring the iPod.** Listening to up-tempo music has been found to increase gains, as does training with a partner. http://bit.ly/ZW8sOz
- **Avoid the scale.** As you put on lean muscle, your weight may increase, since muscle is denser than fat. Stick to your program—results will follow.

It Has Always Been Your Choice

"Vitality—We are alive! The world celebrates with each moment of our mindfulness and gratitude for that awareness."—S. LeBlanc

"There is nothing like returning to a place that remains unchanged to find the ways in which you yourself have altered."

— NELSON MANDELA, FORMER SOUTH AFRICAN PRESIDENT

How exciting it is that we've gotten this far! Being exposed to new levels of mind and body awareness will have an immediate impact. Remember that everything we are experiencing, no matter how significant, expands our perspective, and evolves our consciousness. So consider your consciousness evolved (hopefully).

So what have we learned? We now have a better understanding of:
- how our body works and the impact our actions have on our health
- disease states, and an overview of common diseases
- foods we should focus on, and those we should be wary of
- how toxic our environment has become, and how we can mitigate the damage
- the impact of chronic stress on our health, and ways to reduce day-to-day stress
- the critical importance of sleep, and ways to ensure you give yourself the best chance for a good night's sleep
- the benefits of making fitness part of your daily regimen, and a bird's eye view of how to incorporate fitness into your routine

All this information can be overwhelming if absorbed all at once. Yet, this book isn't meant to add stress to your life. I don't expect you to implement everything tomorrow. It's not about perfection. That would be a recipe for failure. Ideally, you would start with one new habit, then add another, and another. Over time, you'll find that certain nuggets of information will resonate. Tackle these nuggets first. The easier, the better. It has to be at a pace you can manage. If you start slow and continue driving forward, these positive changes will (themselves) become a habit. But in the end, it's all about you making the decision to change.

Focus on the Game Board Instead of the Player

Changing habits can be hard. I'll give you that. It's hard because it takes an extraordinary effort for extraordinary benefit. And one major benefit is the conservation of willpower. Depending on the habits we implement, we may be conserving the willpower previously needed to avoid that muffin, or do that extra set at the gym, or shut off our smartphone in the bedroom. Putting in the hard yards to make something a habit, whether it takes three weeks or three months, will conserve willpower (on a daily basis) for the rest of our lives. Willpower—like a muscle—depletes throughout the day. So the fewer times it's called upon, the greater chance it will be there when we need it most.

Yes, there will be habits that are hard to implement, but if they're worth it, we need to find a way to follow through. We need to change our perspective. Instead of trying to change the player (i.e., you), we need to change the game board, and focus on controlling our environment.

Let's first focus on your bad habits. List the top ten. How easy are they to perform? How easy is it to grab that chocolate bar, or that smartphone, or that late night snack? Is the chocolate bar in the cupboard next to the microwave? Is the smartphone on your night table next to your bed? I think you're getting the picture.

Instead of placing the chocolate bar in the cupboard, (if you need to buy it in the first place) hide it upstairs, out-of-view. Instead of the smartphone being on the night table, shut it off and put it in the guest bedroom. And to help make that late-night snack a little more of an investment to eat, floss your teeth right after dinner.

The point is to make all your bad habits a little harder to perform (i.e., to increase the 'activation energy'). Activation energy is a term used to describe the energy needed for a chemical reaction to occur. When you make it harder to do something, it will take more energy to get it done. So focus on making bad habits a little harder to perform, then a little harder, then a little harder, until it's easier for you to just eliminate them from your routine.

Now for the good habits. Again, list the top ten habits you'd like to implement. How hard are they to perform? How hard is it to make it to the gym, or to meditate for ten minutes, or to have a healthy breakfast? Is the gym fifteen minutes out of your way when you drive home? Do you plan your meditation for late in the day, then run out of time? Is the easiest thing to eat for breakfast a bowl of sugary cereal?

Use the opposite thought process for the good habits, as you did for the bad habits. Instead of needing to hit the gym fifteen minutes out of your way, buy a set of kettle bells, and workout at home. Instead of leaving your meditation for the late evening, get up ten minutes earlier, and do your meditation first thing. And avoid that sugary cereal by organizing your kitchen to make it easier to start your day with a healthy smoothie.

In this case, we're making good habits easier to perform by reducing the activation energy, in effect using less willpower. Everyone is different, so you'll need to match the motivation you need to implement a good habit, with the energy it will take to implement. The less motivated you are, the easier you'll need to make it. It's that simple. The hardest part is making the decision to choose differently.

Take It Easy on Yourself

At times, you'll want to quit. At times, you'll fail. You're in good company because we all fail. This realization makes it easier to practice the art of self-compassion. From a Buddhist perspective, you can't care for anybody before you care for yourself. This provides the best angle to view self-compassion. Imagine how you would treat a child or a best friend, and start treating yourself the same way.

Would you call your child an idiot if they spilled a smoothie on the counter? Would you yell 'f*ck!' if your friend forgot his keys and had to take an extra five minutes to find them? If the answers are no, then how can you justify speaking to yourself in that fashion? I'd always defend my self-deprecation as 'just what I do', and laugh about it. Little did I realize, I was reinforcing deep insecurities and feelings of inadequacy.

Self-compassion is self-esteem without the need to compare us to others, or society's unrealistic ideals. It's about allowing us to make mistakes without judgment.

I'm not suggesting that we shouldn't learn from our mistakes. I'm suggesting that we're allowed to make mistakes. We're allowed to miss a workout, and not obsess over it for days. We're allowed to screw up our diet without feeling compelled to binge-eat because we already 'cheated'.

Simon and Garfunkel have a song with the line, 'I am a rock, I am an island.' Fortunately, most of us aren't rocks. We're fragile and caring beings with imperfections. Embrace the imperfections. Be kind to yourself. Maybe you'll find yourself being more kind to others.

Expect to Fail

There will be plenty of times when you'll need to practice self-compassion, because you will fail... often. The key is to expect to fail. When you do, you'll be ready. You'll realize that each time you fail, it means that you're one step closer to succeeding.

Often, the toughest pill to swallow is failure. It's the feeling of being less worthy, or less of a person because we weren't perfect. This reaction is solely in our mind, and based on expectations.

If we had an expectation that we would lift three-hundred pounds, we'd be disappointed if we fell short. If we had the expectation that we would get that promotion in three months, we'd feel defeated and angry if we got passed over. Expectations. Expectations. Expectations. I can't say it enough.

For most of us, every gauge of our success and worth is based on an expectation. This holds true 100% of the time. Try it. All roads lead to you (or someone close to you) expecting a certain result. You then judge yourself based on that expectation.

Yet, expectations do serve a purpose. They are the basis of goal setting. They help us strive to succeed. They're the barometer we set for progress and growth.

Just don't be blinded and miss the truth that expectations are merely a fictional target you've set. It doesn't have any bearing on your intrinsic worth or how many people love you. It's merely an expectation. That's all. You will be a better individual on the other side, whether you succeed or fail.

Quite frankly one expectation that we should all have is that we will fail repeatedly. We should embrace these failures because without failure there is no growth.

Every single person who has ever walked the earth has failed repeatedly. If it's good for Edison and Einstein, then I would say that we're in pretty good company. As Winston Churchill so aptly stated, "Success is not final, failure is not fatal: it is the courage to continue that counts."

None of our journeys will look the same. There will be missteps, but it's worth it. Every time you fall and get back up, you are conditioning yourself to succeed. All you need to do is get back up and move forward.

The Circle of Life

We've come full circle. I've taken you on a journey to improve your well-being, while masking the underlying motive behind this book. Ostensibly, this book's aim was to help you become healthier, and find your SuperHuman. But finding your SuperHuman is not merely a wellness journey. While I consider a sound mind and body (i.e., physical, emotional, mental, and spiritual health) necessary for happiness, it's not the goal.

To continue to evolve. To continue to strive to reach our potential. To continue to seek out, and live our purpose. Are these not more fulfilling pursuits? Isn't living our purpose what we all strive for? But what does this even mean? What is our purpose?

Each one of us has a unique gift. We have many talents, but only one unique gift. It may evolve over time, but there is something each one of us possesses that no one else does. I believe that the expression of this gift is our purpose.

If you strive to live your purpose, you need a solid foundation. The Buddha stated, "To keep the body in good health is a duty... otherwise we shall not be able to keep our mind strong and clear." Having a sound body and mind is the foundation we need to express our unique gift. I hope I have provided enough of a burning platform to motivate you to take action and move forward.

I don't know your purpose on this earth. Discovering that will take focused work, a high level of self-awareness, the belief that you're meant for something more, and a healthy mind and body. So, I urge you to start this first part of your journey now. Soon you will achieve energy levels and health that you never thought possible.

It's time to Find Your SuperHuman!

Bibliography

175 Tips to Improve Your Training & Quality of Life (Poliquin, Poliquin, 2011)

Ask Coach Poliquin: The Best Q&A Columns From Over Two Decades (Poliquin, Poliquin, 2011)

Forks Over Knives: The Plant-Based Way to Health (Campbell and Caldwell, The Experiment Publishing, 2011)

Foundations of Professional Personal Training (CanFitPro, Human Kinetics, 2007)

In Defense of Food: An Eater's Manifesto (Pollan, Penguin, 2009)

Liver Cleansing Handbook (Natural Health Guide) (Lake, Alive Books, 2002)

More Natural "Cures" Revealed (Trudeau, Alliance Publishing Group, 2008)

Must Have Been Something I Ate (Kotsopoulos, Oceanside Publishing INK, 2011)

Natural Cures They Don't Want You To Know About (Trudeau, Alliance Publishing Group, 2004)

Organic Manifesto: How Organic Food Can Heal Our Planet, Feed the World, and Keep Us Safe (Rodale, Rodale Books, 2011)

Our Toxic World—A Wake Up Call (Rapp, Practical Allergy Res Fndtn, 2004)

Skinny Bitch (Freedman and Barnouin, Running Press, 2005)

The 150 Healthiest Foods on Earth: The Surprising, Unbiased Truth about What You Should Eat and Why (Bowden, Fair Winds Press, 2007)

The China Study (Campbell and Campbell II, BenBella, 2005)

The Cure: Heal Your Body, Save Your Life (Dr. Timothy Brantley, John Wiley & Sons, 2009)

The End of Food (Roberts, Houghton Mifflin, 2009)

The Little Book of Bathroom Meditations: Spiritual Wisdom Everyday (Heller, Fair Winds Press, 2003)

The Metabolic Typing Diet (Wolcott and Fahey, Harmony, 2002)

The Most Effective Ways on Earth to Boost Your Energy (Bowden, Fair Winds Press, 2011)

The Omnivores Dilemma: A Natural History of Four Meals (Pollan, Penguin, 2007)

Wheat Belly (Davis, Collins Canada, 2012)

You: On A Diet: The Owner's Manual for Waist Management (Roizen and Oz, Scribner, 2009)

End Notes

So, What's Broken:
1. American Diabetes AssociationAmerican Diabetes Association
2. Cancer Statistics 2013, American Cancer Society, 2013
3. American Diabetes Association
4. The Economist— December 15, 2012
5. Lazarou J, Pomeranz B, and Corey PN. *"Incidence of adverse drug reactions in hospitalized patients."* JAMA 279 (1998): 1200–1205)

SECTION 1:
Part One: How The Body Works *(Ikkuma Translation: Building The Fire)*
1. Victoria Belt Publishing, 2010
2. USDA Economic Research Service, Food CPI, and Expenditures
3. American Journal of Clinical Nutrition, March 2010; 91 (3): 535–546
4. The Atlantic, "How Vegetable Oils Replaced Animal Fats In The American Diet," April 26th, 2012
5. Staprans I., Rapp J., et al. *"Oxidized cholesterol in the diet accelerates the development of aortic atherosclerosis in cholesterol-fed rabbits"* Jan 1998, Arteriosclerosis, Thrombosis and Vascular Biology: American Heart Association
6. Cromie W., *"Growth Factor Raises Cancer Risk"* April 1999, The Harvard University Gazette
7. Abou-Donia MB, El-Masry EM, et al. *"Splenda Alters Gut Microflora and Increases Intestinal P-Glycoprotein and Cytochrome P-450 in Male Rats"* J Toxicol Environ Health A. 2008;71(21):1415-29
8. P.C. Konturek, T. Brzozowski, S.J. Konturek, "Stress and the Gut: Pathophysiology, Clinical Consequences, Diagnostic Approach and Treatment Options," Journal of Physiology and Pharmacology 2011, 62, 6, 591–599

Part Two: Disease... Know Thy Enemy
1. USA Today, November 17th, 2009
2. The Economist, Dec 15th, 2012
3. Van Straten, Michael. *"Super Detox"* London: Quadrille, 2003
4. Simopoulos AP., *"The Importance of the Ratio of Omega-6/Omega-3 Essential Fatty Acids."* Biomed Pharmacother. 2002 Oct; 56(8):365–79
5. Doll R, and Peto R. *"The causes of cancer: Quantative estimates of avoidable risks of cancer in the United States today."* J. Natl Cancer Inst 66 (1981): 1162–1265
6. Carroll KK, Braden LM, Bell JA et al. *"Fat and cancer."* Cancer 58 (1986): 1818–1825
7. Horio F, Bell RC, et al. *"Thermogenesis, low-protein diets, and decreased development of AFB1—induced preneoplastic foci in rat liver."* Nutr Cancer 16 (1991): 31–41
8. (Schulsinger D, Root M, Campbell T. *"Effect of dietary protein quality on development of aflatoxin B1—induced hepatic preneoplastic lesions."* J. Natl. Cancer Inst. 81 (1989): 1241–1245
9. Biro F, Galvez M, Greenspan L, et al., *"Pubertal Assessment Method and Baseline Characteristics in a Mixed Longitudinal Study of Girls"* Journal Pediatrics, Aug 2010

10. Wu A, Pike M, Stram D. *"Meta-analysis: dietary fat intake, serum estrogen levels, and the risk of breast cancer."* Journal Nat. Cancer Institute. 91(1999): 529-534
11. Colditz G, Willett W, et al. *"Family history, age, and risk of breast cancer. Prospective data from the Nurses' Health Study."* JAMA 270 (1993): 338-343
12. International Agency for Research on Cancer. Globocan 2002
13. Parkin DM, Whelan SL, Ferlay J, et al. *"Cancer Incidence in Five Continents, Vol.I to VIII."* Lyon: IARC 2005
14. Howe GR, Castelleto R, et al. *"Dietary intake of fiber and decreased risk of cancers of the colon and rectum: evidence from the combined analysis of 13 case-controlled studies."* Journal of the National Cancer Institute 84 (1992): 1887-1896
15. American Cancer Society, Cancer Statistics 2013
16. Giovannucci E, Chan J. *"Dairy products, calcium, and vitamin D and risk of prostate cancer."* Epidemiol. Revs 23 (2001): 87-92
17. Akerblom H, Knip M, et al. *"Putative environmental factors and type I Diabetes."* Diabetes Metab. Rev. 14, 31-67 (1998)
18. Dahl-Jorgensen K, Hanssen K, and Joner G. *"Relationship between cow's milk consumption and incidence of IDDM in childhood."* Diabetes Care 14 (1991): 1081-1083
19. Benbella Books 2006
20. *National Diabetes Fact Sheet: General Information and National Estimates on Diabetes in the United States, 2000*. Atlanta, GA: Centers for Disease Control and Prevention
21. Anderson R. *"Deaths: leading causes for 2000."* National Vital Statistics Reports 50 (16) 2002
22. National Heart, Lung, and Blood Institute. *"Morbidity and mortality: 2002 Chart Book on Cardiovascular, Lung, and Blood Diseases."* Bethesda, MD: National Institutes of Health 2002

SECTION 2:

Part One: Foods To 'Live' By *(Ikkuma Translation: Feeding The Fire)*
1. Journal of Nutrition Nov 1990, 120:11S:1433-1436
2. Staprans I., Rapp J., et al. *"Oxidized cholesterol in the diet accelerates the development of aortic atherosclerosis in cholesterol-fed rabbits"*, Arteriosclerosis, Thrombosis and Vascular Biology: American Heart Association. Jan 1998,
3. FDA, Recall of Shell Eggs, October 18th, 2010
4. Gunnars K., *"Pastured vs. Omega-3 vs. Conventional Eggs—What's The Difference?"* March 2013, Authority Nutrition
5. Karsten HD, Patterson PH, et al. *"Vitamins A, E, and Fatty Acid Composition of the Eggs of Caged Hens and Pastured Hens."* January 2010, Cambridge University Press
6. *Too Much Red Meat May Shorten Life Span*, CNN, March 12th, 2012
7. FDA.gov, 2009 Summary Report on Antimicrobials Sold or Distributed for Food-Producing Animals
8. Segal M, Johnson R, et al. *"How safe is fructose for persons with or without diabetes?"* American Journal of Clinical Nutrition November 2008, 88(5): 1189-1190
9. Singh and Fraser, 1998
10. Singh, P. N., and Fraser, G. E. (1998) *"Dietary risk factors for colon cancer in a low-risk population."* American Journal of Epidemiology 148, 761-774
11. EWG, PCBs in Farmed Salmon, July 31st, 2003
12. M. Rodale, Organic *Manifesto*, Rodale, 2010

13. A. Aris, S. Leblanc, "*Maternal and fetal exposure to pesticides associated to genetically modified foods in Eastern Townships of Quebec, Canada.*" Reprod Toxicol: May 31: 528–33
14. American Academy of Allergy and Asthma Immunology, Asthma Statistics
15. L. Szabo, "*Food Allergies in Kids Soar,*" USA Today, Oct. 23, 2008, 7D
16. Gucciardi A., "*GMO Study: Rats Fed Lifetime of GM Develop Mass Tumors, Die Early.*" Natural Society. Sept, 2012
17. Mesnage R, Bernay B, Seralini GE, "*Ethoxylated adjuvants of glyphosate-based herbicides are active principles of human cell toxicity,*" Sept 2012
18. Hardell L, Eriksson M, "*A Case Controlled Study of Non-Hodgkin Lymphoma and Exposure to Pesticides*" Journal of American Cancer Society, March 15, 1999
19. Heitanen, et al., Acta PharmacolToxicol (Copenhagen), August 1983: 53(2):103–12
20. Mercola Dr., "*You'll Probably Accidentally Eat This Toxic Food Today*", 2012 May, http://articles.mercola.com/sites/articles/archive/2012/05/15/california-gmo-panel.aspx
21. Benbrook C.M., "*Impacts of genetically engineered crops on pesticide use in the U.S.—the first sixteen years*", 2012, Environmental Sciences Europe
22. USGS, Irrigation Water Use
23. Garber L., "*New Study Confirms GMO Crops Causing More Pesticide Use, Superweeds,*" October, 2012, Natural Society
24. American Academy of Environmental Medicine, "*Genetically Modified Foods,*" May 8th, 2009
25. Woody T., "*Honey Bees Are Dying Putting America At Risk Of A Food Disaster,*" May 2013, Quartz
26. Rodale M., "*Organic Manifesto,*" 2010 Rodale, pg 149
27. Rodale, 2010
28. Penguin Books, 2008
29. National Research Council. Diet, Nutrition and Cancer, Washington, D.C.: National Academy Press, 1982: 162–165
30. Bjelakovic G, Nikolova D, et al., "*Antioxidant supplements for prevention of mortality in healthy participants and patients with various diseases.*" March 2012, Cochrane Collaboration
31. Moerck Dr. "*Astaxanthin & key carotenoids: creating leading edge eye healthcare formulations,*" Valensa 2013

Part Two: Foods To 'Drive' By *(Ikkuma Translation: The Fire Is Starting To Fade)*
1. Campbell TC and Dunaif GE. "*Dietary protein level and aflatoxin B1—induced preneoplastic hepatic lesions in the rat.*" , The Journal of Nutrition 117 (1987): 1298–1302
2. Jarvis M, "*USDA Issues Final Rule on Organic Access To Pasture,*" February 2010, USDA
3. Willer, Helga; Kilcher, Lukas, 2011, "*The World of Organic Agriculture. Statistics and Emerging Trends.*" Bonn; FiBL, Frick: IFOAM
4. A Schecter, J Startin, C Wright, M Kelly, O Päpke, A Lis, M Ball, and J R Olson "*Congener-specific levels of dioxins and dibenzofurans in U.S. food and estimated daily dioxin toxic equivalent intake.*" Environ Health Perspect 102(11) (1994): 962–966
5. Daxenberger A, Breier BH, Sauerwein H. *Increased milk levels of insulin-like growth factor 1 (IGF-1) for the identification of bovine somatotropin (bST) treated cows.* Analyst. 1998 Dec. 123 (12):2429–35

6. Taubes G. *"Is Sugar Toxic?"*, April 13, 2011, The New York Times
7. Nobili V., Marcellini M., Devito R., et al. *"NAFLD in children: A prospective clinical-pathological study and effect of lifestyle advice."* July 2006, Hepatology www.mercola.com
8. Mercola Dr., *"Aspartame is, by far, the most dangerous substance on the market that is added to foods."* November 2011
9. Abou-Donia MB, El-Masry EM, et al. *"Splenda alters gut microflora and increases intestinal p-glycoprotein and cytochrome p-450 in male rats"* Journal of Toxicology and Environmental Health Part A 2008: 71(21):1415–29
10. Mayo Clinic Staff, Trans Fat Is Double Trouble For Your Heart Health, Mayo Clinic 2011 May

SECTION 3:
Toxins… The Ugly Truth

1. Foss K, *"Clues to the early puberty mystery,"* Health Reporter, March 2009
2. Environmental Medical Research Foundation, 2004
3. Valvi D, Mendez M, et al. *"Prenatal Concentrations of Polychlorinated Biphenyls DDE, DDT and Overweight Children: A Prospective Birth Cohort Study."* Environmental Health Perspectives, October 2011
4. Lordo R, Dinh K, et al. *"Semivolatile Organic Compounds in Adipose Tissue: Estimated averages for the US Population and Selected Subpopulations"* American Journal of Public Health, 1996 Sep; 86(9):1253–9
5. Dellorto D., *"Avoid sunscreens with potentially harmful ingredients, group warns,"* May 2012 CNN
6. EPA, *Nonylphenol, and Nonylphenol Ethoxylates Action Plan Summary*
7. WHO/IARC Classifies Radiofrequency Electromagnetic Fields as Possibly Carcinogenic to Humans, May 2011 Electromagnetichealth.org
8. Hardell, Lennart; Carlberg, Michael; Söderqvist, Fredrik; Mild, Kjell Hansson; Morgan, L. Lloyd 2007. *"Long-term use of cellular phones and brain tumors: Increased risk associated with use for ≥10 years"*. Occupational and Environmental Medicine 64 (9): 626–32
9. Hartley & Marks, 2000
10. *"The FDA Exposed: An Interview With Dr. David Graham, the Vioxx Whistleblower,"* August 30, 2005, by Manette Loudon, Natural News
11. Bignell P, *"Italian court reignites MMR vaccine debate after award over child with autism"* June 2012 The Independent
12. Bertell Dr, Epstein Dr., *"The Dangers and Unreliability of Mammography: Breast Examination As A Safe Effective and Practical Alternative,"* 2001 International Journal of Health Services
13. Pearce Dr, Salotti J, et al. *"Radiation exposure from CT scans in childhood and subsequent risk of leukemia and brain tumours: a retrospective cohort study,"* August 2012, The Lancet, Volume 380, Issue 9840, Pages 499–505, 4 August 2012
14. April, 2011

SECTION 4:
Keeping The Body Tuned-Up *(Ikkuma Translation: Stoking The Fire)*
1. Nordqvist J., *"Lifelong Exercise Significantly Improves Cognitive Functioning In Later Life,"* March 2013, Medical News Today
2. Mayo Clinic Staff, *"Metabolism and weight loss: How you burn calories,"* October 2011
3. Larose Dr, *"Marathons damage the hearts of less-fit runners for up to three months,"* October 2010, Canadian Cardiovascular Congress 2010, Montreal
4. Mercola Dr, *"Boosts Your Hormone by 771% in Just 20 Minutes,"* February 2012, http://fitness.mercola.com
5. Helgerud J, Wang E, *"Aerobic high-intensity intervals improve VO2 max more than moderate training,"* April 2007, *Med Sci Sports Exercise*
6. Foster E., *"Stretching before workouts may weaken muscles, impair athletic performance: studies,"* April 2013, *National Post*
7. Cornelissen, V.A., et al, *"Exercise Training for Blood Pressure: A Systematic Review and Meta-analysis,"* Journal of the American Heart Assoc. February 1, 2013; 2(1): e004473

SECTION ONE PART ONE: HOW THE BODY WORKS

Made in the USA
Columbia, SC
28 February 2018